The Psychopathology
of Serial Murder

The Psychopathology of Serial Murder

A Theory of Violence

Stephen J. Giannangelo

Praeger Series in Criminology and Crime Control Policy
Steven A. Egger, Series Editor

Westport, Connecticut
London

.01003458   60114082

Library of Congress Cataloging-in-Publication Data

Giannangelo, Stephen J.
    The psychopathology of serial murder : a theory of violence /
Stephen J. Giannangelo.
        p.   cm.—(Praeger series in criminology and crime control
policy, ISSN 1060-3212)
    Includes bibliographical references and index.
    ISBN 0-275-95434-X (alk. paper)
    1. Serial murderers—Psychology.   2. Serial murders—Psychological
aspects.   3. Psychology, Pathological.   I. Title.   II. Series.
HV6515.G46   1996
616.89—dc20   96-10437

British Library Cataloguing in Publication Data is available.

Library of Congress Catalog Card Number: 96-10437
ISBN: 0-275-95434-X
ISSN: 1060-3212

First published in 1996

Praeger Publishers, 88 Post Road West, Westport, CT 06881
An imprint of Greenwood Publishing Group, Inc.

Printed in the United States of America

The paper used in this book complies with the
Permanent Paper Standard issued by the National
Information Standards Organization (Z39.48-1984).

10 9 8 7 6 5 4 3 2

For Mom and Dad—
together again

Contents

Contents

Preface

The suggestion and presentation of an original theory is, at best, optimistic and ambitious. To attempt to explain a phenomenon such as the psychopathology of the serial killer could easily be described as overwhelming. However, that is the intent of this book.

The reader must be aware that this book will by no means insinuate an explanation that could be carved in stone. This theory must be considered a starting point, a conclusion based on a limited amount of available knowledge; something to be re-examined and rethought with the passage of time and accumulation of information.

The intent is to observe the available information regarding the serial killer, to dissect and apply the consistencies, and to develop a model of pathology. Observed will be clinical viewpoints, existing theory, socioenvironmental influences, and actual case histories. All these factors and more are critical to this analysis and will contribute to the thinking about this subject.

The serial murderer is examined in the context of the *Diagnostic and Statistical Manual of Mental Disorders*, the reference published by the American Psychiatric Association. This is not to say that this book speaks only to those in the arena of psychology; quite the contrary. The book encompasses the disciplines of sociology, history, biology, psychology, and law enforcement, to name a few, and attempts to reach anyone interested in the development and impact of this particular offender on our society.

This book is organized as a review of current clinical perspectives that could be applied to the psyche of the serial killer (Chapter 2); a discussion of sociological observations and environmental factors in the killers' backgrounds (Chapter 3); a discussion of the synthesis of a preliminary theoretical model of pathology (Chapter 4); the analyses of four case studies in the context of prior assumptions (Chapters 5 and 6); a resulting analysis of an etiological theory (Chapter 7); and a conclusion with observations and suggestions. Future research is also considered.

The reader should note that references to various serial killers will appear throughout the text. For those unfamiliar with a particular case, a brief synopsis of each offender appears in alphabetical order in Appendix A. Therefore, each individual will not be footnoted; they are easily referred to in the Appendix.

The reader should also note that terms in this book are by no means universal. Various writers have very specific usages for concept terms such as *dissociative* and *deviance*, which very well may not agree with others' usage. Several forms of media use certain terms in a completely generic manner, to the point of losing their intended distinctions. For example, many newspapers and other media continue to use the term *mass murderer* in reference to serial killers, while those who study these individuals clearly do not find the terms interchangeable.

Therefore, the reader should direct his or her attention to Appendix B to clarify the use and intention of many of the terms used in this book. They are specifically used within the context of this book's perspective and do not intend to insinuate a universal acceptance of their use.

Acknowledgments

The production of this work would have been impossible without the input of many friends. Certainly, of great help were my advisors at Sangamon State University (now University of Illinois at Springfield), whose comments and suggestions I appreciate. Thank you, Karen Kirkendall, Joel Adkins, and Ron Ettinger.

I'd like to note the technical assistance of Karen Kleinsak, Judy Rodden, and Kim Egger. These are friends whose computer-related expertise kept me from producing this work in pencil. Also of great help in the technical arena was Dale E. Lael, whose graphic and production assistance is appreciated.

I must also mention Mike Giannangelo and Keith Hanson, whose mailings always included a new, helpful reference item.

A special note of appreciation goes to Dani Waller for the arduous task of proofreading some difficult material. Bob Craner, Ken Daugherty, and Irene Kelly-Pasley also deserve thanks for their various contributions along the way.

Finally, I must thank my friend, colleague, and mentor, Steven Egger. Over the past few years, Dr. Egger's influence and guidance enabled me to develop and formulate this work, and I must acknowledge his indispensable role in my efforts.

Part I

The Development of a Serial Murderer

1

Introduction: An Identification of the Offender

We continue to be haunted with the fear that people will remember this killer, even glorify him, for the slaughter of our children.
—Families of victims of Danny Rolling

Serial murder. Rarely a day goes by without a fleeting reference to this expression. It's heard on television, in movies, in newspapers, and in everyday conversation. More average Americans know who Jeffery Dahmer is than Jonas Salk. Everybody's heard of serial killers.

But who are they? What makes a handsome, normal-appearing young law student murder dozens of women? Why does a mild-mannered chocolate factory worker kill, dismember, and cannibalize individuals he found attractive, who came home with him on particular nights? What makes a serial killer kill?

The subject of serial murder has been the focus of an inordinate amount of attention, research, debate, and often exploitation in recent years. The sensationalism and emotional response the subject evokes makes it an easy target for articles, movies, true crime books, yellow journalism, TV tabloids, and other money-making paraphernalia ranging from comic books to trading cards. However, sifting through this avalanche of sensationalism does yield a lining of true research and scientific study that might suggest answers to just who the serial killer is, and why.

The first difficult question is, what exactly is a serial killer? The Federal Bureau of Investigation (FBI) has one definition; various theorists have others. Is it just someone who kills more than one person? A hit man? Is a mercenary a serial killer? What about an abortion doctor? The more the question is asked, the more answers there seem to be.

Many definitions of serial murder are established by specific parameters, such as victimology, geographic location, and killer-victim relationships. Some feel serial killers must reveal a certain pattern or their victims must represent deeply rooted symbolism. Other theories include sex and dominance.

Holmes and DeBurger (1988) listed distinctions they found within a pattern of serial murder. They included almost always a male killer and a female victim; a victim the same race as the killer; a killer whose age is between 25 and 35; no geographic variation in sites; victims of similar status; and a stranger-to-stranger relationship between killer and victim (p. 24). Inasmuch as these variables appeared consistent in their small (44) sample, most of these distinctions are arguable in light of various case histories. For example, while male killer/female victim roles are common, many cases include homosexual male killers and victims. A reasonable modification of this assumption could be male killers and "eligible sexual partner" victims.

Eric Hickey, author of *Serial Killers and Their Victims* (1991, p. 8), feels a serial killer must be defined in the most general of terms, so as not to eliminate offenders by speculation rather than through verifiable evidence. His definition includes "any offenders who kill over time." Hickey's assertion seems plausible for the most part, except that his all-inclusive population is not usable for purposes of this book. Hickey's demographic approach and breakdown are dissimilar from this book in that there are specific offenders excluded from this consideration, by design. The direction of this book is to consider a theory originally formulated by personal speculation, and then to evaluate its merit in the context of verified evidence.

Steven Egger's (1990) definition of a serial killer states:

a serial murder occurs when one or more individuals (males, in most known cases) commits a second or subsequent murder; is relationshipless; is at a different time and has no apparent connection to the initial murder; and is usually committed in a different geographical location. Further, the motive is not for material gain and is believed to be for the murderer's desire to have power over the victims. (p. 4)

Egger's definition also includes a specific consideration of the victims, offering that they may have a symbolic value and insinuating that they are selected often for their perceived vulnerability. The assumptions regarding the serial murderer in this book will more closely resemble Egger's than any other, differing mainly in reduced consideration of victim status and greater concentration on the killer's personality, internal motivators, and development.

The focus here will be on what would appear to be the essence of the phenomenon of this particular criminal. The definition of a serial murderer, which parameters this book will be operating under, will therefore be narrow. There will be an attempt to identify a very specific psychological dynamic, in theory. Mass murderers and spree killers, for example, are not included, as they appear to involve an entirely different set of psychodynamics.

Eliminated are murderers of a serial nature who have any financial or other tangible motivation that might render incidental the killing aspect of the crime. Also eliminated from the study are the cult-obsessed type, as it appears the "true" serial killer—or at least the type this analysis tries to identify—may be drawn to cult activities, but not necessarily. The serial murderer kills because he wants to, not because he is mindlessly led by a cult. This targeted personality may carry out killings in a serial manner owing to an association with a cult, but not because he or she is merely guided or even controlled by that influence. The specific psychological phenomenon to be identified here is a development of internal factors, motivating someone to habitually kill for the implicit thrill, satisfaction, or satiation of the act; or as Herman Mudgett put it: for the "pleasure of killing my fellow beings" (Editors, 1992, p. 95). The ultimate control of another human being and the accompanying catharsis are the psychological hallmarks of the individuals to be discussed.

The reader must understand that the focus of this book is to try to identify and characterize the individual who kills for the joy of killing. Unlike Hickey's broader population, this book will consider a smaller, more focused sample set of data, defined by greater consideration of preliminary information. The examination will be of a group of offenders whose need and motivation to kill appear unencumbered by extraneous variables, such as money or outside influence.

The actual prevalence of this type of offender is difficult to pinpoint. Estimates have ranged from 6,000+ victims a year (McKay, 1985,), to 4,000 a year (Lindsey, 1984,), to 3,500 to 5,000 a year (Holmes and

DeBurger, 1988). Kenna Kiger notes that active offenders have been estimated as low as 30 to as high as 500, depending on the source of research (Egger, 1990, p. 37). These figures represent activity in the United States, as cross-cultural research is extremely limited. There is little agreement, other than the fact that these killers exist and continue to thrive in our society.

The media have called attention to the activities of law enforcement agencies in apprehending the perpetrators of these sensational crimes. Undeniably, these issues are of critical importance and relevance. However, the direction and perspective of this book is psychological, putting forth a "blueprint" of the development and motivation of the serial killer. Discussed here are some of the current theories commonly applied to this phenomenon. These theories are then combined with admitted intuition and speculative insight to develop and consider a theoretical model of the psychopathology of the serial killer.

2

Clinical Diagnoses
and Serial Killer Traits

I am a mistake of nature. I deserve to be done away with.
                                                    —Andrei Chikatilo

CLINICAL PHENOMENA AND THE SERIAL KILLER

Many "syndromes" and clusters of personality traits as recognized by the psychological community are noted in the literature regarding serial killers. The following labels and diagnoses are often assigned to these offenders at some point in their contact with psychologists or psychiatrists, both before and after their crimes. Also, many law enforcement agencies, in studying this type of offender, point to the following characteristics and clinical phenomena in an effort to understand the thought patterns driving these offenders' behavior.

The Antisocial Personality

Most often, serial killers are described as psychopaths or sociopaths, or in more current terminology, as having adult antisocial personality disorder. According to the *Diagnostic and Statistical Manual*, or *DSM-IV*, (American Psychiatric Association, 1994, pp. 649–50), the criteria for this disorder include:

A. Pervasive pattern of disregard for and violation of the rights of others, occurring since age 15 as indicated by at least three of the following:

   1. Failure to conform to social norms with respect to lawful behavior

   2. Deceitfulness, as indicated by repeated lying, use of aliases, or conning others for personal profit or pleasure

   3. Impulsivity or failure to plan ahead

   4. Irritability and aggressiveness

   5. Reckless disregard for the safety of self or others

   6. Consistent irresponsibility, as indicated by repeated failure to sustain work behavior or honor financial obligations

   7. Lack of remorse, as indicated by indifference to or rationalizing having hurt, mistreated, or stolen from another

B. Individual is at least 18 years of age

C. The occurrence of the behavior is not exclusively during the course of a schizophrenic or manic episode

D. Evidence of conduct disorder onset before age 15

These criteria are particularly relevant to the serial killer, as many such offenders share childhoods colored with demonstrations of behavior consistent with conduct disorder, such as aggression to people and animals, forced sexual activity, and fire setting (*DSM-IV*, p. 90). Key elements shared by the sociopath, or antisocial personality, and the serial killer are a failure to conform to social norms regarding lawful behavior, physical aggressiveness, impulsivity, lack of regard for the truth, manipulativeness, and most important, lack of remorse or empathy. Remorse is reported by some serial killers after commission of some crimes, but never to the point of their changing their behavior or seeking help (i.e., Dodd, Nilsen, Dahmer, Bundy, and others).

Causal factors for an antisocial personality include a possible biological predisposition (Andreasen, 1984, p. 252), childhood trauma (shared by the vast majority of serial killers), possible neurological factors in the control of impulsivity regarding serotonin levels in the brain, and heredity. Those diagnosed with antisocial personalities also share deep-seated doubts regarding their own adequacy (Havens, 1992). Most antisocials are men, again reflecting serial killer demographics.

It should be noted, however, it is not enough to simply describe the serial killer as an antisocial personality. The vast majority of the current prison population share this diagnosis, as well as many "average" citizens not incarcerated. Actually, most of us at some time or another could look over the *DSM-IV*'s criteria and recognize a few qualities close to home. This clustering of traits is helpful, however, as it adds to an overall profile and suggests possible consistencies and etiologies, but the criteria should not be overrated.

The Psychopathic Personality

Actually, *antisocial* and *psychopathic* are not interchangeable terms, as commonly used. Psychopathy is diagnosed in about one of three incarcerated individuals and is a far more severe psychological condition in terms of symptoms and treatment. The psychopathic offender appears to be predisposed for predatory violence and is the classic serial killer personality. Indeed, this type of personality was the subject of J. Reid Meloy's book, *The Psychopathic Mind* (1988).

The psychopath, according to Meloy, is a personality incorporating both aggressive narcissism and extended chronic antisocial behavior over time. The personal history of psychopaths shows a trail of used, injured, and hurt people as these individuals tarnish their object world in a continuous effort to build their own fragile sense of self. Robert Hare (1993) noted that psychopaths "have little aptitude for experiencing the emotional responses—fear and anxiety—that are the mainsprings of conscience" (p. 76).

In identifying the psychopath, the revised *Hare Psychopathy Checklist* (PCL-R) (Hare, 1991) measures such traits, most if not all of which are found in the serial killer personality:

1. Glibness and superficial charm
2. Grandiosity
3. Continuous need for stimulation
4. Pathological lying
5. Conning and manipulativeness
6. Lack of remorse or guilt
7. Shallow affect
8. Callous lack of empathy
9. Parasitic lifestyle
10. Poor behavioral controls
11. Promiscuity
12. Early behavior problems

13. Lack of realistic, long-term goals
14. Impulsivity
15. Irresponsibility
16. Failure to accept responsibility for actions
17. Many short-term relationships
18. Juvenile delinquency
19. Revocation of conditional release
20. Criminal versatility

These traits are comparable to those traits found in the antisocial personality, but the checklist goes a step further in identifying internal as well as external characteristics. This clustering is similar to ones observed in Cleckley's *Mask of Sanity* (1941).

The psychopath is more frequently and severely violent than the antisocial personality, and the violence continues until it reaches a plateau at age 50 or so, while nonviolent activity drops off sooner (Hare, McPherson, and Forth 1988). The psychopath is generally regarded as untreatable.

A key aspect of the psychopath in regard to serial killers is that the violence tends to be predatory and primarily on a stranger-to-stranger basis. The violence is planned, purposeful and emotionless. This emotionlessness reflects a detached, fearless, and possibly dissociated state, revealing a lower autonomic nervous system and a lack of anxiety. The psychopath's general motivation is to control and dominate, and his history will show no bonds with others.

Sexually, psychopaths continue their grandiose demeanor and are hypoaroused autonomically, which causes them to be continuously seeking sensation. Their attitude is one of entitlement, not reciprocity. This lack of bonding reflects a lack of emotionality and a diminished capacity for love, where sexual partners are partly objects and are devalued. The psychopath also displays a propensity for sadism (Meloy, 1993).

Borderline Personality Disorder

A comparable condition to antisocial personality disorder is borderline personality disorder, which includes a pervasive pattern of instability in interpersonal relationships, self-image, affects, and marked impulsivity. This pattern begins by early adulthood and is present in a variety of contexts, as indicated by the presence of at least five of the following (*DSM-IV*, 1994, p. 280):

1. Frantic efforts to avoid real or imagined abandonment
2. A pattern of unstable and intense interpersonal relationships characterized by alternating extremes of idealization and devaluation
3. Identity disturbance; markedly and persistently unstable self-image or sense of self
4. Impulsivity in at least two areas that are potentially self-damaging
5. Recurrent suicidal behavior, gestures, threats, or self-mutilating behavior
6. Affective (emotional) instability owing to a marked reactivity of mood
7. Chronic feelings of emptiness
8. Inappropriate, intense anger or difficulty controlling anger
9. Transient, stress-related paranoid ideation or severe dissociative symptoms

Again, this disorder includes a defective sense of identity and extreme instability. The sufferer often views the world as "all good" or "all bad." This description could relate to the large percentage of female serial killers who act as "angels of mercy," who attempt to right the world's wrongs, or who seek revenge and owe the world (or some part of it) a payback. Aileen Wuornos was diagnosed by a prison neuropsychologist as meeting all eight of the criteria for borderline personality disorder (Reynolds, 1992, p. 282).

Though borderline disorder is more often diagnosed in females, it is not exclusively so, as even Jeffery Dahmer was diagnosed by prison psychiatrists as having features of this disorder (Dvorchak and Holewa, 1991, p. 138). Arthur Shawcross also exhibited such characteristics, and John Wayne Gacy was described by a forensic psychiatrist, Richard Rappaport, as utilizing borderline personality organization. Rappaport stated that Gacy brought young boys to his home so he could "star in a play scripted by himself," illustrating a primitive ego defense common to borderlines: projective identification (Cahill, 1986, pp. 339–340).

Causal factors in borderline personality disorder include a history of incest or other sexual abuse and a proneness to experience dysphoria, or a generalized feeling of ill-being, as well as abnormal anxiety, discontent, or physical discomfort, commonly thought to be connected to a problem of the limbeck system.

Both antisocial and borderline disorders display gross deviation from normal attachment processes, which results in a disinhibition of violence (Meloy, 1993). The borderline individual will be pathologically attached, while at the other end of the spectrum is the antisocial, who is pathologically detached.

Dissociation

Another phenomenon usually considered in the psychology of serial murder is the dissociative state or disorder. Dissociation (Egger, 1990) is the lack of integration of thoughts, feelings and experiences into the stream of consciousness. In other words, it is a mental "separation" from the physical place of an individual. Dissociation has been cited as an example of spontaneous self-hypnosis (Bliss, 1986, p. 166). The phenomenon has been used to describe peoples' reactions to various traumatic experiences, as well as a precursor to pathologies described in the *DSM*, such as fugues, amnesias, depersonalization, multiple personality disorder, and post-traumatic stress syndrome.

Morton Prince (1975) referred to dissociative states as:

a large category of conditions characterized by alteration of the personality. In this category are to be found various types of alteration, some normal and some abnormal, all due to the same processes and mechanisms and therefore fundamentally resembling one another, in that they are all types of depersonalization and repersonalization from the standpoint of the modern conception of the structure of the personality. Specifically, these types are known as sleep, hypnosis, fugues, trance, somnambulisms, multiple personality, etc. (p. 291)

Causality regarding dissociative states include severe childhood trauma and some evidence of a physical predisposition. Many of those who experience dissociative states are of above-average intelligence, another trait found in many serial killers.

Literature involving serial killers and the possible presence of a dissociative state is extensive:

Jeffery Dahmer: He couldn't embrace. He couldn't touch. His eyes were dead (Dvorchak and Holewa, 1991, p. 32). *Ted Bundy*: I looked up at Ted and our eyes locked. His face had gone blank, as though he was not there at all (Kendall, 1981). *Dayton Leroy Rogers*: He seemed to be slipping in and out of a fantasy state [while calling the victim someone else's name] . . . he was all-consumed by the deep mental state he was in (King, 1992, pp. 30, 38). *Wayne Nance*: He [the victim] looked him straight in the eye. He saw nothing: no glee, no remorse, just a dead gaze (Coston, 1992, p. 313). *Bobby Joe Long*: It was like a dream me doing it (Norris, 1992, p. 125).

These episodes indicate a certain level of dissociative process, albeit on a minor scale. Usually, the process does not appear as a full-blown dissociative disorder, such as a psychogenic fugue state or multiple personality disorder and does not enter into the psychopathology of the serial killer. These disorders have not been documented or confirmed with any frequency (if at all), and are often the basis for an attempt at malingering or are used as the basis for an insanity defense (i.e., Bianchi, Gacy).

Drawing a parallel between a psychopathic personality and the dissociated demeanor of the serial murderer, Meloy, (1992) noted that "psychopathy is, among other things, a disorder of profound detachment." He added, "from this conscienceless, detached psychology emerges a heightened risk of violence, most notably a capacity for predation" (p. xvii).

Doubling

The discussion of dissociation leads to mention of a recent theory in the psychology of rationalizing killing, that of doubling. Lifton, in *The Nazi Doctors* (1986), refers to doubling as:

the division of the self into two functioning wholes, so that a part-self acts as an entire self. An Auschwitz doctor could, through doubling, not only kill and contribute to killing but organize silently on behalf of that evil project, an entire self-structure (or self process) encompassing virtually all aspects of his behavior. (p. 418)

This "self process" could easily be the phenomenon exhibited when a killer appears to be in a different or detached state, "watching" what is going on rather than being the direct participant, thus removing him or herself from the feelings and responsibilities of murder.

Lifton speaks of the benefits of doubling, including the connection of the two selves. This connection could allow serial killers to put on a "mask of sanity" when not participating in crimes, as well as avoid guilt, which might otherwise be utilized in a typical antisocial personality. Finally, the unconscious dimension of doubling takes place largely outside of awareness, allowing an alteration of moral consciousness. The serial killer who attaches critical importance to his or her acts, and is driven by the fantasy and then the act, can incorporate those acts through this unconscious dimension. It is an active psychological process, a means of adaptation to extremity (p. 422). Robert Ressler, veteran profiler for the FBI, has stated "psychopaths . . . are known for their ability to separate the personality who commits the crimes from their more in-control selves" (1992, p. 154). This sounds very much like Lifton's principles.

James S. Grotstein speaks of the development of a "separate being, living within one that has been preconsciously split off and has an independent existence with independent motivation, separate agenda, etc." and from which can emanate "evil, sadism, destructiveness or even demoniacal possession" (1979, pp. 36–52). He attributes its development to those elements of the self that have been artificially suppressed and disavowed early in life.

The phenomenon of doubling appears to have been observed even by Freud (1938), who coined the term *splitting* to identify dissociation in relation to repression. This was further specified by Kohut (1971, pp. 176–177, 183) by conceptualizing vertical, rather than horizontal, splits in the psyche, noting the "side-by-side existence of cohesive personality attitudes with different goal structures, different pleasure aims, different moral and aesthetic values."

According to Lifton, doubling can include elements considered characteristic of sociopathic impairment, such as a disorder of feelings, pathological avoidance of a sense of guilt, and resort to violence to overcome a masked depression. Murderous behavior may thereby cover a feared disintegration of the self, a concept that appears so critical and so damaged in the view of a serial killer.

Narcissistic Personality Disorder

The *DSM-IV* describes the narcissistic personality as that having a pervasive pattern of grandiosity (in fantasy or behavior), with need for admiration. The pattern begins by early adulthood, and is present in a variety of contexts, as indicated by at least five of the following (1994, p. 282):

1. Has a grandiose sense of self-importance
2. Is preoccupied with fantasies of unlimited success, power, brilliance, beauty, or ideal love
3. Believes that he or she is "special" and unique and can only be understood by, or should associate with, other special or high-status people
4. Requires excessive admiration
5. Has a sense of entitlement
6. Is interpersonally exploitative
7. Lacks empathy
8. Is often envious of others or believes that others are envious of him or her
9. Shows arrogant, haughty behaviors or attitudes

Most of these traits can be found in the serial killer's personality, (i.e., Bundy, Wuornos). Aggressive narcissism is pervasive in the classic psychopath, and features a pronounced sadistic streak (Meloy, 1992, p. 69).

All these features were found in Angelo Buono and Kenneth Bianchi, the "Hillside Stranglers." When asked by a prison inmate why he killed all those girls, Buono brazenly declared, "They were no good, they deserved to die. It had to be done" (O'Brien, 1985, p. 301). Many other witnesses, including even Bianchi, noted one of Buono's favorite phrases was "some girls deserve to die."

Obsessive-Compulsiveness

Another pattern that seems to emerge with serial killers is the presence of obsessive-compulsive traits. Obsessive compulsive disorder can manifest in *obsessions*, defined as recurrent and persistent ideas, thoughts, impulses, or images, experienced at least initially as intrusive and senseless—for example, a parent's repeated impulses to kill a loved child (*DSM-III-R*, 1987, p. 145). Additionally, the thoughts, impulses, or images are not simply excessive worries about real-life problems; the person attempts to ignore or suppress such thoughts or impulses or to neutralize them with other thoughts or actions. The person recognizes these obsessions as a product of his or her own mind (*DSM-IV*, 1994, p. 207).

Also apparent are *compulsions*, defined as repetitive, purposeful, and intentional behaviors performed in response to an obsession, according to certain rules or in a stereotyped fashion. The behavior is designed to neutralize or prevent discomfort or some dreaded event or situation; however, the activity is not connected in a realistic way with what it is designed to neutralize or it is clearly excessive. Also, the person recognizes that his or her behavior is excessive or unreasonable (p. 208).

Similar behavior patterns on a smaller scale (obsessive-compulsive personality disorder) feature a number of ongoing life patterns, such as overperfectionism; preoccupation with details, order, and organization; the unreasonable insistence that others follow his or her way of doing things; indecisiveness; overconscientiousness; and inflexibility. A restricted expression of affection, miserly hoarding of money, and a reluctance to delegate tasks or work with others have also been noted.

Obsessive-compulsive people often have problems expressing aggressive feelings and so they stifle them, causing an implosion of emotions that could cause great internal damage. They often have a history of stress, are usually male, and are often children of people with obsessive-compulsive disorder or personality disorder themselves. The obsessive-compulsive condition often precedes the onset of depression.

Also apparent is a biological link other than the aforementioned heredity. One hypothesis is there are communication difficulties between the brain's frontal lobes and its basal ganglia, buried deep in the lower part of the brain. This creates problems of integrating sensory, motor, and cognitive processes, and results in persistent unwanted thoughts and involuntary actions (Bruno, 1993, p. 147).

It seems that these traits are yet another dimension easily applied to a great number of serial killers, yet are often overlooked by the literature. Consider the obsessive rituals of a David Berkowitz, the compulsive habits of a Dayton Rogers or Robert Berdella, the terror of the "dreaded event" (potentially being alone) of a Jeffery Dahmer. Obsessive-compulsive behavior often shows up in males, and there are strong suggestions of genetic or biological links. Most important, the extreme insistence of these personalities that others follow their rules sounds deadly similar to the emotions of those whose main pathology stem from a need to dominate and control.

A final consideration here is the actual process of completing compulsive acts. First, there is the cycle of discomfort and anxiety, followed by the act (which relieves the tension), followed by a period of guilt and/or a reliving of the act. This process mirrors the apparent cycle of a serial killer's activities: the urge, the act, and the "cooling-off" period. The process can also include postoffense behavior, such as reliving the fantasy that has become reality, getting involved with the investigation, or returning to significant locations (Douglas, et al., 1986).

Post-Traumatic Stress

One final condition to be considered is post-traumatic stress disorder. The *DSM-III*'s opening statement regarding this condition put it to a serial killer's perspective: "The person has experienced an event outside the range of usual human experience and that would be markedly distressing to almost anyone" (1987, p. 146). The *DSM-IV* goes on to note: "The essential feature is the development of characteristic symptoms following exposure to an extreme traumatic stressor"; the person suffers a "markedly reduced ability to feel emotions especially those associated with intimacy" and also shows "diminished responsiveness to the external world, referred to as 'psychic numbing' or 'emotional anesthesia,' usually soon after the traumatic event" (1994, p. 425).

The childhood trauma that all serial killers seem to share, whether it be emotional, physical, sexual, or a combination, would most likely fit the description of a distressing event, serious enough to cause these symptoms. Certainly the dissociative trances of a Jeffery Dahmer or an Edmund Kemper could be interpreted as a post-traumatic response.

Victims of post-traumatic stress often experience recurrent and intrusive distress, as well as dreams, illusions, hallucinations, and as discussed earlier, dissociative episodes. Other symptoms relating to the serial killer are feelings of detachment or estrangement from others, an inability to have loving feelings, a sense of a foreshortened future, irritability, outbursts of anger, and difficulty in concentrating.

INSANITY: AN UNCLEAR CONCEPT

Not mentioned as yet is the possibility that serial killers are psychotic, insane, or simply mentally ill. This may be an issue of semantics, as many will say that anyone who commits atrocities such as savage rape, torture, murder, dismemberment, or cannibalism, surely must be crazy. The idea is that, for one to be able to kill and handle dismembered body parts, the person must be insane. This is commonly referred to as the *res ipsa loquitur* argument—the theory speaks for itself (Masters, 1991).

Some people feel that the insanity defense requirements are purposefully difficult to ensure conviction of violent offenders. Cheney (1992) felt in the Kemper trial "everyone [was] afraid to find out that there was something really wrong with the defendant" (p. 190), and she states that the "disparity between medical and legal definitions of insanity perpetuate a fiction which is bizarre and actually harmful, however soothing to some members of the public" (p. 173).

Those on the prosecution's side will disagree. E. Michael McCann, prosecuting the Dahmer case, drove home this point to the jury: "Committing an unnatural act, such as having sex with a dead body, does not in itself denote insanity" (A horror, 1992). Even the judge at the Dennis Nilsen trial pointed out that "a mind can be evil without being abnormal" (Masters, 1992).

What makes the insanity plea so difficult is it is inherently confusing. "It's an attempt to explain rationally the irrational," says William Moffit, an Alexandria, Virginia, defense attorney (Toufexis, 1992). The legal term *insanity* bears little resemblance to common or even what is considered medical usage. Insanity is, actually, only a legal term, and is certainly not found in a diagnostic manual such as the *DSM-IV*.

Generally, the legal test is whether, at the time the crime was committed, the defendant was suffering from a mental defect that made him incapable of telling right from wrong. Some states also consider whether a defendant's mental illness impaired his or her ability to control his or her actions. The Dahmer case hinged on this "irresistible impulse" defense (Toufexis, 1992).

It is often assumed that the defendant must at least be suffering from a psychosis, not a personality disorder (i.e., antisocial personality disorder, which is usually specifically excluded as a defense), to qualify for an insanity defense. However, a key point to remember is that even the presence of psychosis is not enough. Merely being schizophrenic does not automatically exculpate one from one's actions. It must be proven that the accused's mental condition was the reason for his or her not being able to appreciate the wrongfulness of his or her actions or be "unable to conform his [or her] conduct to the requirements of the law" (Smith and Meyer, 1987, p. 389). However, this is an issue for the courts to decide, mainly because the concept of insanity is purely a legal one.

Very few serial killers are found insane, but some (i.e., DeSalvo, Lucas, Chase, Corona, Kemper) have been diagnosed as psychotic or schizophrenic at some time. Still, the majority of individuals considered in this book appeared to understand the difference between right and wrong and seemed aware of the circumstances and results of their actions.

Ted Bundy, admitting he was well aware of what he was doing, just made reference to the compulsion:

I don't have a split personality. I don't have blackouts. I remember everything I've done. [After one killing] we went out for ice cream after eating hamburgers. It wasn't like I had forgotten or couldn't remember, but it was just over . . . gone . . . the force wasn't pushing me anymore. (Kendall, 1981, p. 175)

Dr. Park Dietz, the widely respected insanity defense expert, noted in a statement following the Dahmer trial:

If the jury had found Mr. Dahmer insane, it would have been open season for sex offenders, because the core of the defense theory was that sexually deviated men cannot control their behavior. . . . [They] are precisely analogous to the disorders found among most child molesters, serial rapists and serial killers, as well as many of those committing sex offenses. (1992a)

SUMMARY: THE CLINICAL PERSPECTIVE

In considering the theories brought out in this section, we can see a pattern emerge. It seems that while serial killers show many syndromes as described in the field of clinical psychology, "there is no single diagnostic category [at this time] that fits these individuals. The pathology of serial murderer is a separate diagnostic category" (Apsche, 1993, p. 10).

Labels such as antisocial, borderline, narcissistic, and psychopath do apply; phenomena such as dissociation, doubling, post-traumatic stress, and obsessive-compulsive behavior can be observed. Many of these states have overlapping features and etiology. There are shared biological or neurological aspects in most cases, indicating a possible physical factor. For most serial killers, there definitely appears to be a history of physical, sexual, or mental abuse. Finally, and possibly most important, these killers seem to evidence a pervasive lost sense of self and intimacy, an inadequacy of identity, a feeling of no control. These could all be factors in a pathology that manifests itself in the ultimate act of control—the murder, and repeated murder, of other human beings.

3

Background and Development of the Serial Killer

They ain't got, I don't think, a human being alive that can say he had the childhood I had.

—Henry Lee Lucas

POSSIBLE ETIOLOGICAL FACTORS

In considering the potential ingredients to produce a serial murderer, the literature includes many phenomena in addition to the syndromes described in the *DSM-IV*. Mental, physical, and sexual abuse; organic damage or biological anomaly; mental and attitude maladjustments; and sexual dysfunction are but some of the other factors that come into play.

This chapter will review the issues that seem to consistently color or correlate with the histories of serial killers. Some issues are included because of an intuitive sense one develops when analyzing the literature; others simply appear too often in these cases to ignore. Here I will focus on the environmental details and social influences on the development of the serial murderer. Unlike Chapter 2, which presented clinical psychology's perspective on the personality types embodied by these offenders, this chapter discusses the personal and social issues in their development.

Biological Perspectives

The notion of nature or biology as a key element in social deviance reaches as far back as criminologist Cesare Lombroso in the late nineteenth century. Lombroso observed the physical correlations between violent ("born") criminals and certain animals, or "beasts of prey." His distinction between the "born criminal" and the "occasional criminal" (one led to criminality owing to illness or difficult situation) marks the predatory nature of the serial killer.

Soon after Lombroso's declarations regarding the inherited nature of criminal tendencies, confirmatory evidence was provided in a book by sociologist Richard Dugdale. Included was a study of a clan led by two sons who married their illegitimate sisters; the results showed that out of over seven hundred descendants, only six did not become prostitutes or criminals. Another sociologist, Henry H. Goddard, studied a soldier who had fathered a baby by a "feeble-minded girl," then married a Quaker of an honest and intelligent family. Nearly five hundred of the Quaker girl's descendants were traced, none of whom were criminals; of the same number of descendants of the feeble-minded girl, only 10 percent were normal (Wilson, 1989, pp. 177–79).

There has been growing research to indicate that aggressiveness and criminality do have a genetic factor (Pervin, 1989, p. 316). Identical twins are twice as likely as fraternal twins to be similar in their criminal activity. A close relationship has also been found between antisocial behavior in adopted children and such behavior in their biological parents.

An analysis of case histories shows a steady pattern of inherited biological and/or physical abnormalities in serial killers. Many such killers, over the course of their abusive upbringings, suffered head injuries and trauma directly—for example, Henry Lee Lucas, Albert DeSalvo, and Bobby Joe Long. Head injuries have been known to cause markedly abnormal personality changes, as well as can affect higher brain functions, such as mediation of instincts (as in rage, aggression, violence, and sexual gratification). The cerebral disturbances of some individuals are detected by neurological signs as temporal lobe epilepsy and electroencephalogram (EEG) abnormalities. John Wayne Gacy is just one serial killer diagnosed with epilepsy. Others exhibit irregular EEGs under special circumstances—for example, after drinking alcohol (Levin and Fox, 1985, p. 31). One killer's abnormal EEG was referred to as a "neurophysiological handicap" that weakened his ability to resist the psychogenetically induced impulse to kill (Revitch and Schlesinger, 1981, p. 22).

There is a striking prevalence of neurological impairment among juvenile killers. In a study done by Dr. Dorothy Lewis, all fourteen of the death row inmates in her sample had a history of symptoms consistent with brain damage, including head injuries severe enough to result in hospitalization and/or indention of the cranium. In addition, serious documented neurological abnormalities such as focal brain injury, abnormal head circumference, abnormal reflexes, seizure disorders, and abnormal EEG readings were found (Ewing, 1990, p. 9).

Another support for the theory of physical abnormality is the presence of behavior clusters commonly referred to as the MacDonald triad. Various researchers have asserted that these behaviors include late enuresis (bed-wetting), fire setting, and animal abuse (Revitch and Schlesinger, 1981, p. 177) as well as other displays of impulse control possibly traced to a neurological origin. Other neurological signals include epilepsy (as in the case of Gacy), dyslexia and other learning disorders.

A classic example is Bobby Joe Long. His congenital dysfunction of the endocrine system caused him to develop breasts at puberty, as well as experience a lunar protomenstrual cycle for life (Norris, 1992, p. 101). Combined with his brain injuries from a motorcycle accident and four other severe head traumas before the age of 10, this condition must have had an impact on his insatiable sex drive, persistent headaches, and violent personality.

It has been said that the predatory behavior of prey animals reflects "a neurological basis that is different from that of other kinds" of behavior (Moyer, 1968). In other words, predatory aggression is different from other aggression, in that it "does not show rage and is not interchangeable with fight behavior, but it is purpose-oriented, accurately aimed, and the tension ends with the accomplishment of the goal" (Fromm, 1973, p. 99). The calm, purposeful behavior of the accomplished serial murderer clearly reflects the actions of a predatory aggressor rather than the behavior of an excited, fight stimulated organism.

The temptation is great to consider a person's history of violence as the main precursor to further violence. However, not every child who is abused becomes a serial killer, just as not every child who is abused develops a multiple personality. Sometimes children in the same family, subjected to the same abuse, take different psychological routes. One may develop a multiple personality and another, although experiencing problems, does not. There is an explanation for these differences, and it appears to be organic.

So, what about the children of killers, of rapists? There are no twin studies to ascertain the behavior of siblings raised in different settings involving violence. However, consider the example of Aileen Wuornos, an alcoholic lesbian slayer of seven. Her father was a child molester, a kidnapper, and a "violent sexual predator" (Reynolds, 1992, p. 257). He was also a bed-wetter until age 13. At one point, he escaped from a hospital for the criminally insane, but he eventually hung himself in prison. When she was an infant, he left Aileen and her 15-year-old mother. Little Aileen must have been her father's daughter. Her Dad may not have taught her anything, but did he leave the seed of violence?

Research on biological factors regarding serial killers was conducted by Richard T. Kraus (1995), in an investigation of the Arthur Shawcross case. Kraus noted that the 47,XYY chromosomal karyotype, abnormally elevated urinary kryptopyrroles, and multiple brain injuries "have relevance as identifiable precursors for potential violence in such individuals with a history of behavioral disturbance."

Jacobs, Brunton, and Melville (1965) initiated the first chromosome survey for XYY males, discovering a high incidence of males with the extra chromosome among a criminal population described as "dangerous and violent." Later studies (Casey et al., 1966; Price and Whatmore, 1967; Court-Brown, Price, and Jacobs, 1968) supported these findings, and concluded that "the extra Y chromosome is associated with anti-social behavior . . . and predispose its carriers to increased risk for developing a psychopathic personality" (Kraus, 1995). Also of interest were findings by Neilsen, et al. (1969; Neilsen, 1970) indicating that XYY patients might be a "comparatively high risk for committing arson, sexual criminality and a high frequency of violence." Price and Jacobs (1970) found that "the behavior disorders in these men which may exist in the absence of mental deficiency . . . correlate with a personality disorder . . . [and] points to the existence of a constitutional psychopathic state."

In case reports of children with XYY, the children are described as "enigmatic in their personality development . . . vulnerable to simple threats and stresses that most would shrug off . . . loners . . . isolationists" (Money, 1970). Zeuthen et al. (1975) found the children with XYY who "grew up in good homes . . . to a certain extent differed from their siblings"; they were "more impulsive, restless, hot tempered, hyperactive . . . and lacked control of aggressive impulses."

Behavioral Genetics (1982) summed it up: "For the XYY, there seems to be little doubt. The extra Y does create some special risk for developing anti-social behavior." These findings all suggest episodes and characteristics in the histories of most serial killers.

Kryptopyrrole (referred to as the *mauve factor*) is an endogenous metabolite that occurs in humans in either very low amounts or not at all. A reading of Arthur Shawcross's kryptopyrrole level revealed the following: "urine kryptopyrrole: H 200.66 mcg/100cc. Expected value 0–20" (Olsen, 1993, p. 491). The H was laboratory shorthand for "high," already evident by the numbers. Shawcross had over ten times the expected highest amount of kryptopyrrole circulating in his body.

When this substance circulates in the body, it forms a stable Shiff's base with pyridoxal phosphate (the aldehyde form of pyridoxine or vitamin B_6) and then complexes with zinc, thereby depriving the body of these two essential compounds (Pfeiffer et al., 1974). Both pyridoxal phosphate and zinc are cofactors at the catalytic site of many enzymes. Decarboxylation reactions normally involve pridoxal phosphate in the synthesis of various neurotransmitters, such as dopamine, norepinephirine, GABA, and serotonin, while zinc is a cofactor in many enzymes, such as lactate dehydrogenase and alkaline phosphate. In addition, both pyridoxal phosphate and zinc are involved in the biosynthesis of heme, which is essential to life (*Harper's Biochemistry*, 1990). As a result, any deficiencies in pyridoxal phosphate or zinc can result in medical illness and psychiatric disturbance (Kraus, 1995).

In a study of the relationships among kryptopyrrole, zinc, and vitamin B_6, Ward (1975) reported that the level of kryptopyrrole can vary in the same individual, increasing when that person is experiencing more stress and falling "dramatically" with large doses of zinc and vitamin B_6 with an associated decrease in stress. Pfeiffer (1974) states that urinary excretion of kryptopyrroles is increased by stress of any kind.

O'Reilly et al. (1965) found that the incidence of this condition was "much higher in emotionally disturbed children and adults than in the general population." A high urinary kryptopyrrole level does appear to correlate with low stress tolerance and loss of control (Kraus, 1995). Thus, it is considered a "biochemical marker of psychiatric dysfunction" and "can identify individuals at high risk for becoming violent."

Kraus's research in the Shawcross case clearly indicates that there are biological markers for psychiatric disturbance and violence. Also indicated is the aggravation caused by stress at all levels. The XYY research is extensive, while kryptopyrrole study is limited regarding serial killers at this time. However, the inference of a biological predisposition is inescapable.

Researchers and geneticists at both Massachusetts General Hospital and the Netherlands found a genetic mutation in some men that was more likely to cause them to be aggressive and violent (Dutch, 1993). Their reports stated that the mutation is associated with abnormal behavior, including attempted rape and exhibitionism (Snider, 1993). They found by urinalysis, the men abnormally metabolized the enzyme monoamine oxidase A, or MAOA. In the brain, MAOA breaks down dopamine, serotonin, and noradrenaline, all substances known to affect behavior. When the researchers examined family genes, the men had slightly different coding from unaffected males.

A 1994 brain-scan study revealed that adults convicted of violent crimes showed impaired function in a key area of the brain linked to impulse control (Elias, 1994). The findings add to the growing evidence that "biological qualities may predispose a person to violent acts." However, Dr. Adrian Raine, a researcher at the University of Southern California, noted "that doesn't mean these brain functions aren't caused by the environment." Dr. Raine said the impairment could be inborn and/or caused by a variety of experiences, including violent shaking by adults in childhood, concussions, gunshot wounds, or even bad falls.

Raine did positron emission tomography (PET) brain scans on 22 adults arrested for murder or attempted murder. Each exam was compared to the scan of a matched adult of the same age but who had never been accused of a violent crime. Findings showed evidence of significantly fewer active cells—meaning lower function in two brain areas crucial to impulse control that are located in the prefrontal cortex. No other brain dysfunctions were found.

Finally, the personality disorders discussed in Chapter 2—antisocial personality, borderline personality disorder, and obsessive-compulsiveness—all suggest some genetic or biological link in serial killers and further underscore the possibility of a physical defect or disposition.

Environmental Factors

Clearly deserving of equal consideration in the development of serial killers is the matter of environmental setting or history. The trauma experienced by the majority of the killers in question is legendary. Consider Albert DeSalvo, who watched his father savagely beat his mother, witnessed the murders of drunks in his neighborhood, and was eventually sold along with his sister to a farmer as slaves. Then there is Henry Lee Lucas, who was forced to watch his mother have sex with various men, was beaten mercilessly daily, was made to eat from the floor, and was brought up as a girl until age 7, wearing long hair and a dress (Egger, 1990, p. 146).

Gerald Stano, who confessed to twenty-five murders of young women in Florida, was linked to at least forty more. He was the fifth child born to a mother who lost all her children to adoption because of abuse and neglect. When Stano was removed from his home, he was malnourished, physically and emotionally neglected, and functioning at an "animalistic" level (Sears, 1991, p. 37).

There are many less dramatic instances of negative environmental settings, but certainly they are abhorrent enough to cause serious damage to a person's sense of self or to development of an appreciation of the lives of others. The beatings that the father of John Wayne Gacy gave him for his suspected homosexuality and underachievement; the practice of Bobby Joe Long's mother making him live in a hotel room with her, sharing her bed; the ridicule and punishment Edmund Kemper received from his mother and grandmother, questioning his masculinity are just a few examples. The combination of physical predisposition and environmental stressors helps develop a pattern of maladjustment with two major consequences: a distorted sense of self and a dysfunctional sexual component.

Esteem Development and Sense of Self

Along with physical abuse, the childhoods of most serial killers are filled with systematic "emotional rape" that harms their impressionable psyches. This injury prohibits them from developing a healthy sense of self, an understanding of intimacy, or feelings of personal esteem.

Childhood is when these killers develop their obsessive and distorted view of their own identities and their ever-increasing need for control. Most have had little, if any, control over themselves or their surroundings as children, and their resulting fear and dread in relation to control issues is understandable, if not predictable.

Many of the personality disorders discussed in Chapter 2 involve a distorted sense of self and a lack of control. These disorders can overlap with other issues, such as fear of loneliness, rejection, overreaction to stress, and misuse of alcohol and other substances.

ıy killers, such as Kenneth Bianchi, David Berkowitz, and Ted
, were adopted early in life. Adoption is sometimes viewed by the
child as the ultimate form of rejection by his parents. Certainly Jeffery
Dahmer's tumultuous upbringing and perceived abandonment set into
motion his loss of self and his immobilizing fear of being alone.

In a 1985 FBI study of sexually oriented murderers (*FBI Law Enforcement Bulletin*), family histories were found to consistently lack a process
for the subjects, as children, to become adults and relate to and value other
members of society. Inadequate patterns of relating as well as infrequent
positive interaction with family members was noted. A high degree of
instability in the home life, as well as a poor-quality attachment among
family members, was also found. Also, interviews showed that most
offenders had unsatisfactory relationships with their fathers, while report-
ing that relationships with their mothers were of "highly ambivalent
quality."

Revitch and Schlesinger (1981) found that, in cases of sexually motivated compulsive gynocide (the murder of women), there was some
unhealthy emotional involvement with the mother. They felt that this
resulted in a displacement of affect from mother to other women, culminating in a displaced matricide (p. 174). They also quote Freud, who stated
that "the sexual instinct itself may not be something simple, that it may
be on the contrary, be composed of many components, some of which
form perversions. Our clinical observation thus calls our attention to
fusions, which have lost their expression in the uniform normal behavior"
(p. 175). Revitch and Schlesinger note that in sadistic gynocide there is a
fusion of sex and aggression.

The Sexual Component

A consistent factor in the development of the serial killer is the
presence of a seriously dysfunctional sexual orientation. This is another
issue given varying degrees of importance by different researchers.
Some feel it is a key influence while others view it as merely incidental.
The position of this book is that deviant sexual motivation clearly has
an impact on the killer's psychology, that it is the bridge, the clearest
link between mental and physical processes in the psychopathology in
question. Dr. David Abrahamson maintains that in "all of what we call
senseless or aimless violence, there is a strong sexual element" (Cheney,
1992, p. 210).

Westley Alan Dodd, the child killer and rapist put to death in Washington state, was certainly on his way to a successful career as a serial sex killer. In his 1992 self-written pamphlet to parents, teachers, and children to warn against people like him (*When You Meet a Stranger*), he claimed to have molested about twenty-five boys and girls and attempted forty others. Albert DeSalvo's uncontrollable sex drive seemed to fuel his mania, as he committed an estimated two thousand sexual assaults (Leyton, 1986, p. 123). Most killers' "careers" are launched by violent sexual fantasies that lead to the sexual assault preceding the actual murders.

Some murderers do not overtly kill with the potential of sexual activity, either pre- or postmortem, being a factor, however, other fetishes and sexual paraphilia are usually apparent. Ted Bundy had an abnormal collection of socks and once stated the importance of having more socks than he could ever use. This reflected the foot fetishes of Dayton Rogers and Jerry Brudos, both of whom severed the feet of some of their victims for later enjoyment.

Not to be forgotten is the motive of pure sexual sadism. Sadism, torture, and rape are usually thought of in terms of violence, but the sexual aspects of these crimes should not be overlooked. Freud referred to sadism as a partial drive of the libido, and explained that sadistic desires have no overt connection with sexual strivings, but are unconsciously motivated by them (Fromm, 1973, p. 280). Quite often the crimes of the a killer enmesh the violence and sexual excitement of the sadist.

Edmund Kemper was described as a pure sadist by one psychiatrist, a condition presumably fueled by his hatred of his mother. DeSalvo seemed to strike out at women who represented the cold rebuke of his wife, Irmagard. Angelo Buono was a seasoned pro at brutal rape before his first murder for pleasure. Even Richard Ramirez noted in an interview (*Inside Edition*, 1993) that his sexual satisfaction could be reached only through violence.

However, sadistic "specialists" such as Lawrence Bittaker and Roy Norris just tortured and mutilated for the sheer enjoyment of hearing their victims scream. Bittaker and Norris wanted to stock their own private town of young girls to torture and rape. Herman Mudgett killed just to "hear their cries for mercy" (Editors, 1992, p. 95). Dayton Rogers even stopped attacking one victim who ceased screaming and resisting, apparently because she took the whole pleasure out of the act.

Albert Fish was so enthralled with sexual sadism and masochism that he regularly inserted needles in his groin, along with engaging in various other forms of self-mutilation. He looked forward to the electric chair as the "supreme thrill, the only one I haven't tried" (Editors, 1992, p. 99).

Sexual sadists have displayed interest in activities consistent with the serial murderer, such as:

selection of strangers as victims; advance selection of a location to which the victim is taken; participation of a partner; careful planning (including impersonation of a police officer); use of a pretext in approaching victims; keeping victims captive . . . sexual bondage . . . performing multiple sex acts . . . intentional torture; murder or serial killings (most often by strangulation); concealing victims' corpses; recording offenses; and keeping personal items belonging to the victims. (Dietz, Hazelwood, and Warren, 1989)

There is also the violent homosexual, who combines the components of a decayed sense of self and sexual urges. Homosexuality and issues of gender identity are considered causes for concern in the *DSM-IV* only when they cause the individual persistent or marked distress about his or her sexual orientation or "other traits related to self-imposed standards of masculinity or femininity" (American Psychiatric Association, 1994, p. 249). Killers who are fueled by a rage and a hatred of their own sexuality include sexually inadequate or homosexual individuals such as Dean Corll, Westley Dodd, John Wayne Gacy, Larry Eyler, possibly Jeffery Dahmer, and Dennis Nilsen. They are prime examples of such violent expression of frustration and rage.

Patrick Kearney, referring to younger homosexuals as "hustlers and phonies," admitted to killing at least thirty-two young men and boys, ranging from ages 5 to 28. He butchered them for years, later at a rate of one per month, and earned the nickname the "Trash Bag Killer" for his disposal methods of dumping the severed remains in garbage bags (Cartel, 1985, pp. 145, 147). Forensic psychiatrist Richard Rappaport echoed observations of personal rage between killer and victim when he noted that "a serial killer often has an extremely close relationship with his victims. He sees in them characteristics he sees in himself " (Garelik & Maranto, 1984).

Lucas, Toole, Bianchi, Buono, Long, Bittaker, Norris, Dahmer, Bundy, Shawcross, Gacy, Corona, Dodd—the list goes on endlessly of serial killers whose primary interest included some form of sexual activity. A current theory is that rape and sadism are not acts of sex but of violence. In some extreme cases, acts of torture, rape, necrophilia, and other deviant paraphilic activities may be labeled as acts of violence, but must also be recognized as acts, however distorted, of sex.

Causative aspects of a sexual deviance, usually including some form of paraphilia or sexual activity with a nonconsenting partner (i.e., rape, exhibitionism, pedophilia), can reflect common psychological characteristics. Social isolation, low self-esteem, and feelings of sexual inadequacy can indicate an emotional immaturity (Costello and Costello, 1992, p. 272).

Sadistic tendencies can sometimes be traced to an early association of emotional feelings in response to someone's inflicting pain, or even torturing an animal. When the experience is a vivid, haunting one, the result may link the inflicting of pain with sexual arousal. Masochism seems to be triggered by early experiences of extreme pain linked with strong emotion, which in some way is associated with a satisfying sexual event (Costello and Costello, 1992, p. 269). Consistent with a diathesis-stress model (see Chapter 4), a predisposing biological component or personality trait must be assumed to cause such events, however powerful, to have lasting effects.

Certainly the dimension that separates these criminals from "ordinary" rapists is the eventual killing of their victims. The act appears far more significant than just a way to cover up a crime or silence a witness. Instead it was for the expressed pleasure and catharsis of the act itself, whether to dominate, to control, or, as Ted Bundy put it, "to possess them . . . forever."

Fantasy

A deviant and consuming fantasy appears to be the fuel that fires the process. Serial killers seem, at an early age, to become immersed in a deep state of fantasy, often losing track of the boundaries between fantasy and reality. They dream of dominance, control, sexual conquest, violence, and eventually murder. Fantasy would seem to be the place where the killer retreats in a dissociative episode.

Jeffery Dahmer, in psychiatric interviews, revealed that he fantasized how it would feel to attack a jogger and "sexually enjoy him" (Dietz, 1992b). He thought out his plan of stalking someone in a certain place and subsequently went there with a baseball bat in rehearsal of his plan.

At an early age, Edmund Kemper also had fantasies of killing his sisters and other people. He extensively fantasized and carefully rehearsed, going through the motions of picking up hitchhikers before he would eventually carry out his homicidal impulses. Dahmer and Kemper's activities are examples of Prentky et al.'s (1989) idea of "rehearsal fantasy," a motivator which is practiced in the environment. This rehearsal fantasy is usually associated with dysfunctions such as genital and gender dysphoria (a general feeling of unhappiness and anxiety regarding sexual issues), experienced by both Dahmer and Kemper. It is in the fantasy where the serial killer determines his future victims' "goodness of fit," a mental representation of the type of individual needed to fulfill a particular pathological need.

Many studies have supported the role that fantasy plays in motivating the serial murderer. The Prentky et al. (1989) study, in which samples of serial vs. single sexual murderers were compared, postulated the role of fantasy as an internal drive mechanism for repetitive (serial) acts of sexual violence. The study's hypothesis was that three items common to serial offenders would be manifested by the existence of a drive mechanism, described as an intrusive fantasy life. They included a high prevalence of paraphilias, documented or self-reported violent fantasies, and organized crime scenes. All three hypotheses were supported by the study.

MacCulloch, Snowdon, and Wood (1983) found "a pattern of sadistic fantasies that, in repetition-compulsion fashion, were played out repeatedly—initially in fantasy only, later on in behavioral mock trials, and eventually in assaults. The more the fantasies were cognitively rehearsed, the more power they acquired." They found that "once the restraints inhibiting the acting out of the fantasy are no longer present, the individual is likely to engage in a series of progressively more accurate 'trial runs' in an attempt to enact the fantasy as imagined."

The genesis and pervasiveness of such fantasies may result from a failure to master the impulses stimulated by child abuse and trauma, hence the repetitive and compulsive nature of both the fantasy and the serial sexual violence (Grossman, 1991).

Burgess, Hartman, and Ressler (1986) found a fantasy-based motivational model for sexual homicide. Interactive components included impaired development or attachments in early life; formative traumatic events; patterned responses that serve to generate fantasies; a private, internal world consumed with violent thoughts that leaves the person isolated and preoccupied; and a feedback filter sustaining repetitive thinking patterns. In this study, they found evidence for daydreaming and compulsive masturbation in over 80 percent of the sample, in both childhood and adulthood.

In terms of classical conditioning, Abel and Blanchard (1974) noted that "the repeated pairing of fantasized cues with orgasm results in their acquiring sexually arousing properties." This is consistent with Bandura's (1969) finding that at least three social-learning variables may be important in linking sexual arousal to deviant fantasy: parental modeling of deviant behavior in blatant fashion; repeated associations between the modeled deviant behavior and a strong positive affective response from the child; and reinforcement of the child's deviant response (Prentky et al., 1989).

John Campbell, of the FBI's Behavioral Science Unit, feels that the media promote fantasy. "We're seeing more serial killers in society because we promote violence through media coverage. The problem with all this attention is that it could have a tendency to foster fantasy—and trigger action" (Davids, 1992). Fantasy's role in the serial murderer's life is providing "an avenue of escape from a world of hate and rejection" (Hazelwood and Douglas, 1980).

Given a scenario in which a person has developed no real sense of self, no concept of esteem or self-worth, and no meaningful reciprocal relationships with those around him, he's likely to see an avenue of escape from hate and rejection. In this person's fantasy, he may remake the present, the past, the future. He may create a world of acceptance and respect. He can enjoy the status of a worthwhile person and be a desirable sex partner. Most important, he can call all the shots, write all the lines, fill in all the blanks. The carte blanche control offered in the world of fantasy is priceless—and addicting.

It appears that many serial killers often retreat into their world of fantasy at some point in their developing pathology. They may delve into sexual, violent, graphic scenarios and use pornography or detective magazines to assist their creative process. Linked with continued masturbation, retreat within themselves, and self-imposed isolation, they begin down the path of a murderous obsession. Fantasy is also a logical first step toward a dissociative state, a process that allows the serial killer to leave he stream of consciousness for what is, to him, a better place.

Jeffery Dahmer had sexual fantasies about corpses and open viscera during a formative stage in his life (Dietz, 1992b). John Joubert fantasized about strangling and eating his baby sitter when he was age 6 or 7, following established patterns of open masturbation and fantasy about strangling and stabbing young boys in their undershorts (Ressler, 1992, p. 120). Monte Rissell was described by a school principal as always "lost in fantasy" (Ressler, 1992, p. 88). Dodd, Kemper, Berkowitz, Rogers, and Nance—the stories of their fantasies are endless and all-inclusive.

Dr. James T. Reinhardt (1992) described the role of fantasy:

> By fantasy the murderer attempts to wall himself in against the fatal act, while at the same time qualifying the compulsive psychic demands in the development and use of fantasy. These sadistic fantasies seem always to precede the brutal act of lust murder. These fantasies take all sorts of grotesque and cruel forms. The pervert, on this level of degeneracy, may resort to pornographic pictures, grotesque and cruel literary episodes, out of which he weaves fantasies. On these, his imagination dwells until he loses all contact with reality, only to find himself suddenly impelled to carry out his fantasies into the world of actuality. This is done, apparently, by drawing some human objects into the fantasy. (p. 208)

The serial killer has often lost himself in a world of fantasy, a world where fantasy is omnipresent and he cannot discern what is fantasy and what is reality. This psychodynamic makes possible the continued execution of violence, sadism, and murder for personal satisfaction. Fantasy can also be seen as a reason that the serial killer can calmly and methodically dehumanize his victims. He then reconnects with the real world (Bundy's live-in girlfriend referred to his "using me to touch base with reality") and carries on immediately after the crime with such seemingly mundane activities as going out for hamburgers (Kendall, 1981, p. 175).

Pornography and Causation

A logical question, after the subject of fantasy is, what role pornography plays. There are those who feel pornography is a causative precursor in the actions of a serial killer. One FBI study showed that, of the sexual/serial killers surveyed, 81 percent listed pornography as their primary sexual interest. The study also noted that the killers were "characteristically immersed in fantasy." A North Carolina State Police study found that 75 percent of defendants in violent sex crimes "had some kind of hard-core pornographic material" in their homes or vehicles (Mellish, 1989).

Dietz, Harry, and Hazelwood, (1986), have suggested that detective magazines contributed to the development of sexual sadism, that they facilitate sadistic fantasies, and that they might serve as training manuals and equipment catalogs for sex criminals. Ted Bundy's claims that he was a victim of pornography, made just before his execution, are well documented. Even Andrei Chikatilo, with pictures of naked women in his holding cell, blamed pornography as the "cause of his troubles."

What of it? Most researchers say that a correlational relationship does not prove anything, much less cause and effect. It would seem reasonable that persons who are so obsessed with sex and fantasy would have pornography in their homes, much as any sports fan would have *Sports Illustrated* or *The Sporting News*. But does pornography or detective magazines incite someone to murder—someone who might not otherwise? Not likely. It should also be noted that Bundy and Chikatilo's credibility in this matter must be considered suspect. Durham (1986)—in response to feminist assertions that pornography is harmful, incites violence, and should be regulated—noted that "the use of unsupported assertions, the limited generalizability of the social-psychological experimental research, the inability of the research to measure the magnitude of the effects of pornography and the failure to conduct the discussion in comparative terms severely undermines the persuasiveness of the argument."

The matter of pornography deserves a study of its own. However, it would that appear pornography is to the serial killer as gasoline is to the arsonist. Both are tools of the sexual criminal. Both are immersed in fantasies and have the motivation to fulfill their erotic desires. Magazines and movies definitely help "fuel the fire." However, without gasoline, the arsonist still finds a match. Without the pornography, Ted Bundy would have killed scores of women anyway.

Lesser Crimes

Obsessive fantasizing, it appears, usually results in a feeling-out period, a time when lesser crimes are committed. Just as in experimentation with fire or animal torture while still a child, the fledgling serial killer usually tries the lesser roles of arson, burglary, theft, sexual deviance, molestation, and assault. Criminal journals are full of Bundys, Dahmers, and DeSalvos who worked their way up the ladder of antisocial acts and behaviors, petty crimes, and control-seizing acts on their way to habitual homicide.

The role of lesser crimes is especially important, as the crimes are usually sexual in nature. These acts—most often arson, breaking and entering, sexual assault, or burglary—represent sexual gratification and control. Though on a smaller scale, these crimes appear to reflect the basic motivations of the serial killer. For example, criminal profiler Diana Sievers (1992) of the Illinois State Police stated that breaking and entering or burglary is an example of the individual gaining the control that he seeks. Even clearly mentally ill or "disorganized" offenders such as Richard Chase committed earlier crimes such as breaking and entering, defecating on a child's bed, and urinating on clothing in a drawer—all "signs of classic fetish burglaries" (Ressler, 1992, p. 16).

William Heirens committed his first killings, he says, because the victims walked in on him while he was in the act of committing burglaries described as sexual in nature. Heirens's murders were categorized by Ressler as a "continuation of the burglaries and other crimes he committed earlier in his teenage years" (p. 50), and he continued to commit many more in between the murders. Danny Rolling was serving four life sentences in Florida State Prison for a series of armed robberies and home burglaries committed in Gainesville, Ocala, and Tampa, at the time of his conviction for the murders of five college students (Abdo, 1994).

Heirens's and DeSalvo's countless burglaries, or Berkowitz's arsons (1,488 in New York—he kept a diary—as well as his pulling several hundred false alarms) are lesser crimes with no motivation other than getting a sexual charge and seizing control.

An Issue of Control

The serial murderer is hard to dissect, even on paper. Factors such as sadism, fear, sexual perversion, emotional maladaptiveness, mounting anger, and hostility apply in different degrees to different offenders. The one constant here, however, is control. Control—whether it be sexual, sadistic, revengeful, or any of the other mindsets held by the killer—seems to be the underlying drive and is the source of the serial killer's motivation and direction to "possess them . . . forever." As Levin and Fox (1985) have noted,

In large part, the pleasure and exhilaration that the serial killer derives from repeated murder stem from absolute control over other human beings. As Roy Norris admitted . . . "the rape wasn't the important part, it was the dominance." (p. 68)

This link between control, rape, and serial murder was also noted by Egger (1985) and West (1987). It was West who pointed out that "it may take only a small increase in the desperation of the assailant or resisting victim to convert a violent rape into a murder" (p. 19).

Indeed, from the earliest inklings of the pathology to come, serial murderers seem to deal continuously with issues of control. The late enuresis (bed-wetting) in their pasts is a control issue that is hard for them to ignore. Dr. Joseph Michaels, a pioneer in the analysis of the correlation between enuresis and murderous behavior in children, explains "Persistently enuretic individuals are impelled to act. They feel the urgency of the moment psychologically, as at an earlier date they could not hold their urine" (Ewing, 1990, p. 11). The biological implications of lack of impulse control, as previously discussed, plus repeated incidence of such "poor impulse control" reflect this position.

The prevalence of animal abuse also appears to be a combination of sexual or sadistic urges and control and dominance needs. The literature is again replete with stories such as that of Wayne Nance, who demonstrated his superiority by dropping kittens into an incinerator or skinning them alive. What easier way to act out your control, which is sorely lacking in real life, than by a skinning a cat or mutilating another defenseless creature? The next logical step is to move on to other objects of easy dominance, such as little girls and boys, women, and other potential victims.

Three teenagers arrested for the brutal murder and sexual mutilation of three 8-year-olds, had combined ritual and animal abuse as they skinned, cooked, and ate a dog. One of the young killers noted to a priest that he had already committed himself to hell, and he couldn't change that (Castaneda, 1993a and b).

This control-centered triad of early crimes includes arson, which is also very common in serial killers' pasts. Arson has distinct sexual features and represents the actions of taking control of the situation, both in fire setting and in pulling false alarms. Shawcross, Berkowitz, and many other serial killers shared this interest.

Control seems to be the underlying motivation for the personality types discussed in Chapter 2—the antisocial personality, the psychopath, the borderline personality, and the narcissistic. They all crave control, whether it is to build a fragile ego or to demonstrate how weak everyone else is. Even necrophiles acknowledge the importance of control. In a clinical analysis, when asked what their primary motivation for necrophilia was, the subjects often said "total acceptance of the subject [victim] . . . the completely unconditional positive regard and total acceptance" (Meloy, 1993).

Erich Fromm (1973), in considering necrophilia, postulated that there is a natural development from the anal, control-obsessed personality, to the sadistic character, and finally to the necrophilous character. He felt that this development was determined by an increase in narcissism, unrelatedness, and destructiveness, and that necrophilia can be described as "the malignant form of the anal character" (p. 349). He also said that the relatively small number of necrophiles were severely pathological cases and one "should look for a genetic predisposition" for this (p. 367). Dr. Ashok Bedi, after examining Jeffery Dahmer, agreed with the connection between necrophilia and control. In regard to Dahmer's necrophilia, he commented:

His personality disorder, the alcohol addiction, the pedophilia, the necrophilia, his ego and homosexuality, all were layers of his dysfunction. The preoccupation of having sex with the dead person had to do with his feelings at different points in time. A living person could not fill his need. Only a dead person, where he was totally in control and there was no way of retaliation, belittlement, negation or abandonment. It was not so much being sadistic as wanting to be in control. Then it became a question of what he was looking for—nurturing, wanting to be fed, that sort of thing. If there was a need to show anger, then he might use anal sex. It depended on what his needs were in his head at the moment. (Davis, 1991, p. 264)

When considering the issues of control and sadism, J. A. Apsche (1993) noted:

When, in children, control is substituted for intimacy [as manipulation and control substituted for closeness], the child mistakenly learns that control is a substitute for intimacy. For the sexual sadist, there is a need to take control to demonstrate power and virility. The mode of death selected is one which indicates that the victim had meaning for the killer, and that the intimacy in the murderous act is part of the close bond between the murderer and the victim formed in the killer's fantasies and delusions. (p. 117)

Erich Fromm, in searching for the "nature of sadism," stated that there were different forms of sadism, and they were not independent of one other. In observing what he called the common element, he wrote:

The core of sadism, common to all its manifestations, is the passion to have absolute and unrestricted control over a living being, whether an animal, a child, a man, or a woman. To force someone to endure pain or humiliation without being able to defend himself is one of the manifestations of absolute control, but is by no means the only one. . . . Complete control over another human being means crippling him, choking him, thwarting him. . . . The person who has complete control over another living being makes this being into his thing, his property, while he becomes the other being's god. (1973, p. 289)

Edmund Kemper summed it up: "I wanted the girls for myself as possessions. They were going to be mine; they are mine" (Cheney, 1992, p. 171).

THE FIRST KILL

The first kill is often the clumsy, inexperienced, and impulsive act of a "virgin" to homicide. Reminiscent of the adolescent fumbling in a car's back seat, David Berkowitz made a botched attempt at stabbing his initial victim. It caused him to eventually change to an easier and more efficient method of shooting his prey.

Sometimes the first kill is the result of what began as a rape or assault, but crossed the line as the frenzy of the episode unfolded. The excitement of the moment made the killer cross the threshold separating fantasy from reality. In other instances, a stressful event in the killer's life triggers an escalation of activity, from crimes such as burglary or rape, to murder. Some offenders may even develop a pattern of increased homicides coinciding with peaks of stress in their personal lives.

Occasionally, killers will say that they do not even remember the details of their first kill, while showing extraordinary memory and clarity for subsequent conquests. Their initiation to murder is often followed with guilt, fear, and reflection, similar to the aforementioned adolescent's first time with sex. The shame and acknowledgment that a grave crime has been committed is felt along with the excitement and the "rush" that comes with the realization of having finally discovered what they truly need. This is also a time to enjoy mental reenactments. As time passes and fear of reprisal fades, these offenders enjoy renewed confidence in their ability to practice their habit undetected. The initial cooling-off period is reinforced within the cycle, and will become part of the dynamics of habits to come.

THE COMPULSION AND RITUAL OF SERIAL MURDER

The completion of the cycle, culminating in the murders, accompanying sexual activity, and postoffense behavior, illustrates the killer's obsessive-compulsive behavior and ritualistic actions.

Albert DeSalvo spoke of the indescribable compulsion that came over him when he strangled (Frank, 1967, p. 378). Increased anxiety about and discomfort with the compelling urge to kill becomes consuming. The eventual killing provides the expected release and satiation, dissipating the tension and introducing momentary relief. Like the addict, the killer will search for the same level of high as experienced during the first kill, but may settle for the release of built-up anxiety. According to the FBI's Robert Hazelwood, "Serial offenders generally commit their crimes as stress is building on them. The stress level reaches a peak, and that's when they make the kill. It's like a weight being lifted off their shoulders" (Coston, 1992, p. 278).

This cycle of anxiety, discomfort, urge, act, and cooling off reflects a similar sequence of emotions and actions cycling within those suffering from obsessive-compulsive disorder or sexual paraphilic obsessions and compulsions, such as exhibitionism. In this case, the urge to kill is obsessive-compulsive.

The times between killings may vary, according to a number of factors. Sometimes there are no victims to meet the killer's criteria, sexually or otherwise. For example, Andrei Chikatilo's killings dropped off in the winter months owing to cold weather. Jeffery Dahmer reportedly refrained from killing a couple of young victims because he didn't have enough time to go to work. Joel Rifkin went months without killing because apparently his "examining trophies—the credit cards, panties and jewelry of previous victims—may have been enough to satisfy him" (Eftimiates, 1993, p. 234).

However, the obsession remains and does not stay dormant long. When one of Westley Dodd's young victims asked him "Why are you doing this to us?" he responded: "Because I have to do it" (King, 1993, p. 288). An example even more illustrative of this compulsion comes from of Ted Bundy:

I have a sickness . . . a disease like your alcoholism. You can't take another drink and with my sickness. . . . There is something . . . that I just can't be around. . . . I know it now. . . . There is something the matter with me . . . I just couldn't contain it. I've fought it for a long, long time. . . . It got too strong. I tried, believe me, to suppress it. That's why I didn't do well in school. My time was being used trying to make my life look normal. But it wasn't normal. All the time I could feel the force building in me. (Kendall, 1981, pp. 174, 176)

Bundy's live-in girlfriend, under her pen name Elizabeth Kendall, appreciated the comparison to her own pattern of alcoholism:

I didn't pretend to understand or accept Ted's compulsion to kill beautiful, vital young women. But I do understand something of compulsion, and I do understand something of what it feels like to repeat compulsive actions over and over again, even though the intention is to never do it again. In my case it was getting drunk repeatedly when I didn't want to. In Ted's case it was so much worse. (1981, p. 177)

At this point it would appear that the killer settles into a pattern of cyclical murderous acts, becoming more and more comfortable in his practices, also gaining efficiency and skill in technique and execution. However, the compulsion and ritual of the kill retains its importance. Wilson and Seaman (1991) observed in regard to Jack the Ripper, "the ritual was of supreme importance to the Ripper. More than that, it was a clamorous, overpowering need, a compulsion, which overruled all other considerations that night—personal safety included" (p. 37). They also noted, regarding an 1809 female killer, Anna Zwanziger, that "as if the need to kill was an addiction, Zwanziger told the judge it would have been impossible for her to cease poisoning others and described the virulent poison as her 'truest friend' " (p. 49).

Ritual was clearly important to Ed Gein, the inspiration for serial killer characters in several movies, who

robbed corpses and body parts from a number of graves. Gein used these limbs and organs to fashion ornaments, such as a belt of nipples and a hanging human head, as well as decorations for his house, including chairs upholstered with human skin and bed posts crowned with skulls. A shoe box containing nine vulvas was but one part of Gein's collection of female organs. On moonlit evenings he would prance around his farm wearing a real female mask, a vest of skin complete with female breasts, and women's panties filled with vaginas in an attempt to recreate the form and presence of his dead mother. (Levin and Fox, 1985, p. 4)

Part of the ritual often includes keeping diaries, photo albums, and other visual aids for reenactment of the crimes. Westley Dodd, along with a categorically detailed photo album, kept a graphic diary of his activities and plans, including descriptions of experiments to perform on the dead (and the living), murder methods, and plans for creating a torture rack.

Robert Berdella, a sadistic rapist and murderer of six, kept skulls, an envelope of teeth, and hundreds of pictures of young men being raped and tortured. He cut up the bodies to be put out with the trash. An excerpt from his diary included this page (Jackman & Cole, 1992, p. 97):

7:30	Bar
	Ferris [victim]
9/26	Drug
9:00	Out
9:05	Shoes + socks off, move arms snoring no rea
9:10	Test need no react [needle]
	2 1/2 cp left a "
	3 cp right a "
9:20	Photo, clothes off, no react
9:40	Turned over, slight arm movement
9:50	Fing F no reac [finger sex]
	1 1/2 cc ket arm no rea
	Front F no react
10:15	BF no reac [anal sex]
10:30	tied arms
10:50–11:00	Carrot F
	Slight resist
	1 1/2 cc cp nk
11:00	2 cc cp vein
11:30–11:45	BF, cub F, slight react
	Regag
12:00	Fightin

The notes continued for two more pages. The top of the third page was marked "Fri," and the last two entries read:

11:45	Very delayed breathing, snoring
12:00	86

The kills become increasingly intense, lessening the effect of a "fix" for this addict of death. Also experiencing shorter cooling-off periods, the obsessed killer may get sloppy (i.e. Dahmer, Bianchi, Rifkin) or more frenzied (Bundy) as time goes on. Some killers, such as Kemper and DeSalvo, say they reach the point when they could have stopped. This might seem plausible for a Kemper, who finally destroyed the object of his rage (his mother), but it is highly unlikely for seasoned serial killers to walk away from their compulsive patterns. Indeed, frenzy, compulsion, sadism, and ritual were all reflected in the words of one of history's first serial killers, Jack the Ripper:

I left nothing of the bitch, nothing. I placed it all over the room, time was on my hands, like the other whore I cut the bitches nose all of it this time. I left nothing of her face to remember her by . . . I thought it a joke when I cut her breasts off, kissed them for awhile. The taste of blood was sweet, the pleasure was overwhelming, will have to do it again. It thrilled me so. Left them on the table with some of the other stuff. Thought they belonged there. They wanted a slaughterman so I stripped what I could, laughed while I was doing so. Like the other bitches she ripped like a ripe peach. . . . One of these days I will take the head with me, I will boil it and serve it up for my supper. (Harrison and Barrett, 1993, p. 102)

Occasionally, serial killer's run comes to an end purely by chance, such as with a routine traffic stop, in the case of Ted Bundy. Most recently, Joel Rifkin, who was pulled over for running a stop sign, was discovered carrying a woman's decomposing body in the rear of his truck. He quickly confessed to the killing of seventeen women (Man reportedly, 1993).

In the vast majority of the cases, however, serial killers will kill until they are caught, by law enforcement efforts, through their own self-destructive misstep, or when they meet their own death. This cheery observation is tempered, however, by the fact that we can never know how many multiple murderers might have killed, then ceased on their own and were never apprehended.

Part II

Toward Development of a Theory of Violence

4

Theoretical Discussion

I will not allow too much time before my next. Indeed, I need to repeat my pleasure as soon as possible.

—Jack the Ripper

PRELIMINARY IMPRESSIONS

In suggesting a pattern for the synthesis of the serial killer, the literature makes reference to many phenomena: the incidence of mental, physical and sexual abuse; the possibility of organic or biological damage or predisposition; prenatal stress; and the development of mental and attitude maladjustments as well as sexual dysfunctions. With consideration of the potential of variables, the result appears to be an inclusive dynamic: all factors acting in concert. The serial murderer's personality develops through a combination of specific variables that feed upon themselves, creating a feedback loop for the activity.

The concept of an interactional dynamic is not without precedent. Eric Hickey (1991) suggested an interactional, sociodevelopmental model he called *Trauma Control*, emphasizing the importance of social structure and stressing the influence of a traumatic event, or *triggering mechanism*. The interactional dynamic presented here is similar, but the key element is a biological component, that is at least equal to environmental factors.

The Diathesis-Stress Model

The theory proposed in this book is a *diathesis-stress model*, a systems approach similar to what is currently offered in the psychological literature for conditions such as schizophrenia. There certainly is a social, environmental factor—or trigger; most obviously it is the extreme psychological trauma suffered by the vast majority of serial killers. This alone, however, is not enough. There seems to be an additional component—a physiological, biological ingredient that makes the mix an explosive one.

Simply put, the diathesis-stress model combines of both nature and nurture. Neither a biological factor nor an environmental situation alone seem to be enough to produce the offender type in question. A biological predisposition acts in concert with a traumatic environmental situation.

The diathesis-stress (*diathesis*: biological; *stress*: environmental pressure) model was first postulated by Gottesman and Shields in 1982. The term refers to a genetic predisposition being a necessary condition, but not sufficient in itself (Lewine et al., 1990). Hans and Marcus (1987) studied a process model for schizophrenia in diathesis-stress terms, underlining the importance of factors such as constitutional vulnerability—that is, biological and genetic risk via family history; early neurobehavioral signs marking a constitutional defect; stressful childhood environment, particularly family environment; and early premorbid childhood signs of poor social adjustment. Their model for etiology "included a constitutional, possibly genetic vulnerability, aggravated by environmental, most likely familial, stresses." It is strikingly similar to the histories of many serial killers, and forms a reasonable theoretical position for this particular psychodynamic.

Silverton et al.'s 1988 study suggested that "genotype may depend on the interaction between genetic factors and environmental trauma. . . . It may be important to consider neuroanatomical sensitivity as an etiological factor . . . in genetically vulnerable persons." Further studies by Walker, Downey and Bergman (1989) made specific note of the effects of child mistreatment and the incidence of violence. Considering the fact that child mistreatment is more common among psychiatrically disturbed parents (Sloan and Meyer, 1983), a genetic and biological basis could be inferred from later exceptionally violent behavior.

Jaffe et al. (1986) found that boys exposed to family violence showed adjustment problems comparable to those manifested by abused boys—conditions reminiscent of many serial killers' histories. The Walker, Downey, and Bergman study suggested that genetic risk interacted with maltreatment in its effects on aggression and behavior. Over time, the acting-out behavior of high-risk children from maltreating families escalated. It appeared that stressful environments may have acted to trigger externalized behavior in their high-risk (genetically predisposed) subjects.

When examining the histories of children who are severely abused, yet do not develop conditions such as schizophrenia or become serial killers, it would appears logical to assume that this abuse—found so regularly and predictably in the pasts of serial killers—must interact with an unknown factor in a lethal manner.

Significant Environmental Issues

Given the diathesis-stress model, environmental triggers must be substantial and noteworthy especially when compared to an "average" upbringing. The factors that consistently surface in reports of these troubled pasts must be recognized as indicators in a progression and become elements of this developmental concept.

These prominent elements (or markers, if you will) include antisocial, possibly criminal acts in youth; a pervasive sexual dysfunction causing great impact and/or stress in the person's life; and dissociative episodes or chronic escapes to fantasy.

Antisocial activity is a somewhat broad category representing the lesser crimes most serial killers bring with them to their first murder. These include fire setting and animal abuse, along with burglary, breaking and entering, and assault. As discussed in Chapter 3, many of these crimes have control and sexual themes.

The extended discussion of *sexual dysfunction* in Chapter 3 clearly explains the inclusion of this factor in the diathesis-stress developmental theory. It is considered an essential ingredient of the serial killer, and offers insight into some other activities he commits peripheral to the murders.

Dissociation and *fantasy* are factors of enormous weight. Time and time again, offenders' stories are colored with dissociative episodes and life in fantasy worlds.

THEORETICAL ANALYSIS

Case Study Method

This book will present case studies as a means to consider the preliminary impressions gleaned from the clinical and social literature. The case
study is the "preferred strategy when 'how' or 'why' questions are being
posed, when the investigator has little control over events, and when the
focus is on a contemporary phenomenon within some real-life context"
(Yin, 1984, p. 13). This describes this book's analysis of the serial killer
and his development in society. In the remaining chapters, case studies
will be reviewed in the light of two assumptions described in the next
section. The elements of each theory will be considered and discussed.

Observational Direction

There are two assumptions considered in this analysis. First, there is a
real, recognizable set of behaviors capable of being observed and categorized, much like the antisocial personality described in Chapter 2, which
can be called a serial killer. *Serial killer* is a label used quite loosely and
without accepted definition at this time. The assumption here is that this
term can be applied to a reasonably consistent diagnosis using a specific
set of parameters.

Second, offenders qualifying for this diagnosis do, for the most part,
conform to the theoretical model and its elements discussed herein. The
offender suffers a combination of predisposition and life stress much like
the schizophrenic, displays a history of early antisocial behavior and
obsession with fantasy and/or flights from reality, and endures serious
sexual dysfunction.

Clearly, there is no one single cause-and-effect factor issue regarding
the serial killer, and a systems-type model must be examined as the sum
of its parts. The critical features of this theory, such as biological components and incidences of trauma, can be measured only with a systematic
examination of a representative sampling of the literature. This does open
the analysis to concern, mainly regarding the correlational nature of such
a study and its inherent lack of proof of cause and effect. However, the
readers should note that this study does not measure the occurrence of one,
peripheral, possibly isolated item such as pornography. The theory postu-
lates a combining, cumulative dynamic—one previously suggested and
favorably tested with regard to other mental conditions, such as schizo-

phrenia. This theory simply goes one step further, noting the propensity of violent offenders to have genetic abnormalities and serial killers to suffer environmental traumas.

Further, although the correlational nature of this study does not necessarily prove causation, a "high correlation occurring would strengthen the credibility of the hypothesis in that it has survived a chance at disconfirmation" (Campbell and Stanley, 1963, p. 64). Given the number of variables within the theory under consideration, high correlation would legitimately indicate the presence of a condition, clinically recognizable as the serial killer, much as it does the antisocial or borderline personality.

The case-study analysis is an appropriate method of examining this theory, considering the limited population of subjects available. Small numbers of hard data would result in minimal statistical validity, weakening a quantitative analysis. Sproull (1988) noted, "In some research projects it is not feasible or desirable to carry out experiments which often intrude on the natural setting, are perhaps more costly or perhaps [when] subjects are not available in a laboratory situation. The research problem still needs to be explored but under nonexperimental conditions" (p. 149).

Also, much of the available information could be deemed second-hand and occasionally anecdotal. This could cause problems in what Denzin (1978, p. 225) refers to as the *reality distance* problem, leading to errors from translation and interpretation. Indeed, it is this anecdotal dimension that weakens much of the research. Even the actual guilt of some killers could be brought into question—for example Albert DeSalvo. According to one retired New York policeman, another suspect may have killed as many as twelve of the thirteen DeSalvo admitted to murdering (2nd Boston, 1993).

Other problems include a built-in weakness regarding external validity, in that some information comes from convenience samples of incarcerated individuals or other reactive subjects, such as victim and offender family and relations.

Finally, ecological validity might be compromised by the manner in which killers speak after being apprehended as opposed to how they respond while engaged in their crimes and when unconcerned with consequences. Researcher Howard S. Becker observed incarcerated criminals "are no longer operating under normal circumstances; they now respond to vastly different controls, and in particular may think by telling their story in one way or another they can use the researcher to influence the authorities on whom their fate depends. They may tell only 'sad stories,' self-justifying tales of how they got where they are" (Denzin 1970, p. 87). Clearly, the most challenging aspect of this material is judging credibility and using multiple sources for comparative analysis and interpretation. Errors and biases must be considered and guarded against.

However, this ex post facto qualitative analysis does allow review of a theory that is intuitive in nature and deals with a subject difficult to translate into qualitative data. This naturalistic inquiry allows for simplified understanding of variables (*coherence conditions*) that may well develop simultaneously with the inquiry, rather than prior to it (Lincoln and Guba, 1985, p. 49).

Lincoln and Guba also note that "the output of naturalism often is a locally grounded theory" and "such theories typically take the form of pattern theories" (p. 49). They quote Reason, a researcher familiar with pattern model theory: "The pattern model involves a number of phenomena all of equal importance, then explaining the connections between them" (p. 49). Lincoln and Guba argue that theories commonly emerging from naturalistic inquiries are of a form (pattern theories) well understood by philosophers of science.

This analysis is a step away from a pure grounded theory, in which a model is developed as a result of continuous evaluation of the literature. It has been, as Egger (1990) put it, "continually shaped and reshaped from analytical interpretations and discoveries," and "shaped intentionally from the data rather than from preconceived, logically deduced theoretical frameworks" (p. 138). The diathesis-stress aspect of the model presented here could be considered grounded theory, yet it is but part of a larger picture.

The theory presented here is appropriately described as intuitive and developed from personal insight, stemming from accumulated study and a review of the research and literature. Glaser and Strauss (1967), said: "An insight, whether borrowed or original, is of no use to the theorist unless he converts it from being simply an anecdote to being an element of theory" (p. 254). This being the case, the preliminary theory presented here must be considered by analysis measuring the elements of the model and through examination of the case histories.

ELEMENTAL ANALYSIS

The assumptions outlined earlier and the correlational approach described provide the basic structure for analysis of the case studies. These studies must be viewed from a consistent vantage point, considering the existence of the aforementioned elements of the theory.

First, is there evidence of physiological anomalies in the subject's history? Analysis will apply the biological component of the theory to see if there is evidence of distinct physiological differences, whether congenital or induced by trauma.

Second, is there evidence of severe environmental trauma in the subject's history? This consideration will pertain to abuse, either emotional or physical, severe enough to markedly disturb the individual or affect personality development.

Third, has the subject evidenced clinically antisocial behavior from an early age and/or committed lesser crimes prior to his first murder? This question looks for activities such as the MacDonald triad, as well as other behaviors that might mark the subject as "different," possibly dangerously, from an early age. It also seeks incidences of criminality prior to the subjects' first serial murder.

Fourth, has the subject ever evidenced problematic sexual deviance? As mentioned earlier, this is an element viewed with varied importance among researchers. However, it is a critical aspect of this book's theoretical basis. The analysis simply regards the history of violent sexuality, problematic homosexuality, or other sexual paraphilic motivations or desires that might be tied to later predatory behavior.

Fifth, has the subjects shown evidence of dissociative episodes? The examination will look for a historical propensity to live in a fantasy state or to be lost from reality for noticeable periods of time, most often by more than one observer.

Finally, has the subject committed predatory murders of a serial nature? This question simply asks if the individual falls within the strict parameters of this analysis. It could be said that this reduces the serial killer to what Gibbons (1987) called an *offender typology*. Gibbons was concerned that this caused an "oversimplified characterization of the real world of criminality" (p. 219). However, the serial killer diagnosis is reasonably clear and explicit enough to be able to assign the offender to a distinct typological category, which can be explored and substantiated through research efforts and not be considered oversimplified.

5

Case Studies

What I wanted to see was the death, and I wanted to see the triumph, the exultation over the death.

—Edmund Kemper

SELECTION OF CASES

A total of four case studies will be reviewed. These cases have been selected mainly for their ease in availability and completeness of material. Their names and span of killing include:

Name	Span of Killing
1. Andrei Chikatilo	1978–1990
2. Arthur Shawcross	1972–1988
3. Jeffery Dahmer	1978–1991
4. Edmund Kemper	1963–1973

I resisted the temptation to include Aileen Wuornos in the group, because changing the homogeneity of the subject population would confound the issues being studied. The population sample for female killers is limited, therefore an unreliable basis for drawing any conclusions.

These cases are well documented and reasonably complete. They also represent a time period ranging from the 1960s through the 1990s. The sample was limited to four so as to allow proper examination of each case; four has been the workable number of cases for comparable studies (see Egger, 1985).

These subjects have all proved to be receptive to interview. Interviews of the subjects as well as of family and friends, are an integral step in assembling a complete historical picture; indeed, these subjects' interviews offer a depth of information. At the time of this analysis, all of the subjects were still alive and all had freely admitted their crimes, paving the way for personal introspection of their motivations and outside observation of their personality development.

CASE 1: ANDREI CHIKATILO

Andrei Chikatilo has been labeled by some as the most prolific serial killer of modern times. The Russian accumulated at least fifty-three murders to his credit, while the ferocity and pure sexual sadism he inflicted on his victims was hard to imagine.

Chikatilo, born in 1936, was raised during the squalor and famine of the Stalin regime. He and his sister, Tatyana, were told a horrific tale of the fate of their brother, Stepan: that he had been captured and eaten. His father had been captured by the Nazis during the war, and placed in a work camp, which for Andrei proved to be a source of shame and rejection by those around him.

Andrei retreated to the safety of his own mind, all the while suffering the continual taunts of schoolmates for his ineptness, often the result of terribly poor and uncorrected eyesight. Dressed in rags, he had no friends and often clung to his mother's side, another trait which usually exacerbated the torment from other children.

Chikatilo married and had two children, a wonder in itself considering his aversion to "normal" sexual activity. It took a great deal of effort and patience for his wife, Fayina, to lead Andrei through the traditional sexual act, as his interests were of a different kind. Chikatilo soon embarked on a long career of molesting young children, losing jobs, and moving around as a result. He also had an interest in prostitutes, who helped him practice his more hard-core proclivities, but it was the children—along with the torture, capture, and fear he could inflict—that excited him.

Andrei committed his first murder in 1978, stabbing to death a 9-year-old girl after an unsuccessful attempt at rape. This murder resulted in the forced conviction of an erroneous suspect, who, sadly for him, had a past which included the murder of a teenage girl and whose semen type matched the specimen found at the Chikatilo murder scene. The suspect was executed five years later.

Another change of jobs required Chikatilo to travel, and suddenly his interest in predation fit nicely with his daily habits, offering a convenient excuse for travel and stays away from home. He would meet victims at bus stops, earn their trust, and take an eventual walk in the woods—always with the same result—violent death and carnage. He killed males and females of different ages, the important point being that they were powerless and easy prey. His need for inflicting fear and pain painted his attacks, as he dismembered, cannibalized, stabbed with frenzy, raped, and masturbated at the scenes of his slaughter.

Finally, in November 1990, Citizen X, as he came to be known, was apprehended, ending a reign of terror his society had never experienced. Chikatilo attempted many defenses, ranging from claims that he was influenced by dirty pictures and videos to assertions of insanity, complete with examples of the proper bizarre behaviors to support his charade. After a six-month trial he was found sane and guilty and was sentenced to death.

Physiological Factors

Chikatilo's background information times mentions head trauma, although this is unproven. Interviews commonly include stories of beatings of the head, but these reports are spotty and unspecific. In 1984 he received treatment for dystonia.

Chikatilo reported a history of severe headaches, although these also are unsubstantiated. His mother supposedly had a history of the same problems.

His blood type of AB was originally mistakenly analyzed as A, because the B antigen is not clearly defined in his blood; it was contained in his saliva, sweat, and hair. This condition greatly confused the authorities during the investigation, as his odd sperm and blood type are found in only 1 in 20,000 people. This condition was not even considered until a medical team from abroad published findings regarding this rare anomaly in late 1988 (Krivich and Ol'gin, 1993, p. 205).

Andrei Tikachenko of the Serbski Institute in Moscow, who analyzed Chikatilo for two months, noted various physiological problems. He observed impotence and attributed certain urges to prenatal brain damage. He also noted a familiar trait—bed-wetting until age 12 (Solotaroff, 1993).

Evidence regarding other biological issues, especially chemical details and genetics, is incomplete. The fact that the killer was in Russia, and these types of studies were not routinely considered, left much unexplored. However, the biological considerations cannot be overlooked, whether they are predispositions or developed after birth. The fact is that other members of his family, as well as neighbors who shared his background, did not grow up to be serial killers. This observation, is of course, intuitive and is based on weakly substantiated correlations.

Environmental Trauma

Chikatilo's background of trauma, witnessing "blown-apart children" and "gathering the corpses . . . in pieces" (Krivich and Ol'gin, 1993, p. 113), as well as the sheer squalor and poverty of his youth, would certainly justify his experiencing symptoms of post-traumatic stress syndrome. He would clearly qualify as one who experienced an exceptionally damaging upbringing.

The experience that appears to have had the greatest impact was hearing the harrowing tale of his older brother, who was said to have been kidnapped and eaten. Instances of such happenings were true in this area during this time. The story is unconfirmed, but even if Chikatilo only believed it to be true, it still would have had a devastating effect. In fact, Chikatilo's psychiatrist, Aleksandr Bukhanovsky, felt that his story of cannibalism, real or imagined, was the main factor that led him to his crimes as a cannibal killer.

Another significant factor stemmed from the muscular condition suffered by his younger sister, which "caused her rectum to fall out of her anus." Chikatilo "spent his prepubescent years haunted by the sight of her and their mother stuffing it back in" (Solotaroff, 1993).

His childhood was seriously flawed. He was relentlessly mocked and ridiculed by his peers for his shortcomings in school and the embarrassments of his family. His young life was spent friendless. Chikatilo's own rationale was that he, before he became a criminal, "was first a victim" (Krivich and Ol'gin, 1993, p. 143).

Early Antisocial Behavior and Prior Crimes

Chikatilo's early crimes of child molestation (his "pink period"), during which time he discovered his preference for sadism, was the very beginning of his developing pathology. His sexual deviance culminated in his committing the largest number of confirmed kills by any serial killer to date. This statistical distinction is likely the result of law enforcement agencies' inability to catch him, however, rather than any particular skill or psychological aspect of his personality.

His early crimes included fondling and injuring a girl in a boarding school where he worked, costing him his job. This was all it cost him, unfortunately, as he eventually ended up in a teaching position and repeatedly made advances to young students. He also accosted his own 6-year-old niece. He knew from the outset that young children excited him, however he was yet to learn the sexual thrill of eliciting cries of help and inflicting pain. Only after his rape and first murder of a little girl in 1978 did he "understand how to satisfy his own lust" (Krivich and Ol'gin, 1993, p. 173).

Problematic Sexual Deviance

Chikatilo's sexual problems began with his inability to sustain an erection during normal sex and the discovery that orgasm could be reached only after infliction of sadistic pain, coupled with the act of coitus while the victim was in the process of dying. It is hard to determine whether his sadism was driven by rage over the inability to consummate a normal sexual act, or his ineptness was caused by a lack of interest in nonviolent sex. His only conventional sexual relationship with a woman was with a mistress he took while married, a former wife of his brother-in-law.

His interests before developing a taste for sadism focused on children; he was "irresistibly drawn to children." He wanted to "see their naked bodies, their sexual organs" (Krivich and Ol'gin, 1993, p. 77). However, after his first murder, he realized that blood aroused him and that nothing else would satisfy him sexually. He was excited by inflicting pain and often had orgasms while the victims were in the final spasms of death. His actions were clearly sexually deviant:

Chikatilo boiled and ate sawn-off testicles or nipples of his victims, or carved slits in some corpses to use for his own brand of necrophilic sex, often not bothering to kill his trussed teen-age victims before the butchery started. . . . The cutting or biting off of male genitals and the excision of a female uterus was followed by a chewing of the organs. Uteruses, he said later, "were so beautiful and elastic." (Martingale, 1993, pp. 135, 140)

He was actually described not just as a sadist but also as a necrosadist. "He needed to see his victims die to achieve sexual satisfaction," wrote Dr. Aleksandr Bukhanovsky. "His killings were an analogue to sexual intercourse" (Cullen, 1993, p. 126).

Dissociative Episodes

Chikatilo had often been described as detached and removed, which could suggest a dissociative process. It would seem closer to doubling, given his remarkable memory for detail in the majority of the murders. Chikatilo's ferocious sadism during the crimes would resemble Grotstein's description regarding doubling in Chapter 2: that Chikatilo displayed "evil, sadism, destructiveness and even demoniacal possession" while wearing the mask of sanity as husband, father, and grandfather. Also, comments from Chikatilo himself, such as "I'm alone in my fantasies, my daydreams" (Krivich and Ol'gin, 1993, p. 115) and "I fantasized my whole life and sometimes couldn't tell my fantasies from reality" (Lourie, 1993, p. 230) reveal a preference to remain within himself.

Others in his life agreed. Fellow employees stated that "his head was in the clouds" and "he was not all there." During meetings in the director's office, he sat in silence, staring off into space or yawning (Krivich and Ol'gin, pp. 187–88). Even when he taught school, students and colleagues alike noted his listless, detached manner, snapping out of daydreams saying, "What was I talking about?" He could "stand silently, for almost an entire class session, rocking slightly to and fro with his hands clasped behind his back" (p. 162).

Serial Murder

Chikatilo's well-documented history of fifty-three murders committed in a predatory, methodical manner easily qualifies him as a serial killer within the parameters established for this study. All his killings appeared to be driven by a desire to commit the act and relieve the accompanying pressure and sexual tension. The acts continued for years and it appears would have done so indefinitely, if not for his eventual capture.

Other Observations

Chikatilo's history reflects the clinical observations of serial killers. Obviously, his murderous activities over the course of thirteen years would suggest obsessive-compulsiveness, along with his rituals after each crime. Also, his "signature" wound inflictions (eye and genital mutilation), although not discussed in this paper, are quite consistent with FBI profiles of serial killers. He escalated in frenzy and sadism:

Not only had he tormented the boy with knife pricks on the throat and chest, not only had he inflicted wounds after death . . . not only had he taken the genitals and wounded the eyes, this time he had opened the body and ripped out the heart with his bare hands. (Lourie, 1993, p. 179)

Chikatilo most definitely suffered from a defective mental capacity, however the trial court's decision in finding him sane and responsible for his actions appears correct. This is evidenced most clearly by his ability to hold back his killing for a two-year period while he knew "they were looking for him." He could not claim being unable to control his actions, as he managed to refrain from killing as frequently in cold months, when it was more difficult and uncomfortable.

In further testimony to his planned behavior, he always carried his knives with him when he traveled, an obvious predatory behavior. He did display some suggestion of paranoia, but it is hard to discern the true pathology needed for an insanity defense at this point.

His skill level reflects that of prior killers, as his first crimes were committed "cautiously, nervously and ineptly," while later ones were "handled with more finesse and resolve" (Krivich and Ol'gin, 1993, p. 190). The crimes increased in their ferocity, and as discussed previously, did not appear to have an end in sight at the time of his capture.

CASE 2: ARTHUR SHAWCROSS

Arthur Shawcross, dubbed the "Genesee River Killer," terrorized the city of Rochester, New York, with a series of eleven killings over a two-year span beginning in February 1988. He was finally captured, as he was observed revisiting a corpse at the site of one of his murders. He was convicted and sentenced to 250 years in prison without parole.

His history includes grisly stories of violence and cannibalism while serving in Vietnam. His erratic, abusive relationships with his mother and family, along with personal sexual problems, clouded and affected his development throughout his early and adult life.

Shawcross committed two child-sex murders and was in prison for seventeen years. Regrettably, and against the protests of his parole officers and other prison officials who had examined him, he was released, only to continue his habits of rape and murder. He then practiced against powerless adults and added cannibalism to his crimes.

His case is an interesting study in the consistent nature of the serial killer. He was profiled by the FBI during his New York rampage, and the profile fit almost perfectly—with one flaw. The FBI estimated his age at mid to late twenties; Shawcross was 43. The difference was the seventeen years of prison. When he was released, he picked right up where he had left off in his late twenties.

Physiological Factors

From a biological standpoint, Arthur Shawcross may be the best researched serial killer. The research conducted by Robert Kraus, cited in previous chapters, is extensive and conclusive in its position that Shawcross had a different biological makeup from most men. The discovery of his genetic (XYY) coding, elevated kryptopyrrole reading (ten times the normal amount), abnormal EEG, readings and head traumas all have clear links to violence and impulse control.

Kraus also noted that Shawcross's kryptopyrrole level correlated to:

partial disorientation, abnormal EEG's, general nervousness, depression, episodes of dizziness, chest and abdominal pains, progressive loss of ambition, poor social performance and decreased sexual potency all found in the history of Arthur Shawcross. Other correlates were "marked irritability, rages, terrible problems with stress and anger control, mood swings, poor memory, violence and antisocial behavior." (Norris, 1992, p. 306)

While in prison Shawcross displayed severe scars on his arms, caused by apparent regular self-mutilation, something often found in borderline personality cases. He was also diagnosed with a prostate ailment.

As a child he experienced many head traumas, including being hit in the head with a stone, an injury that caused periodic bouts of childhood paralysis. He was hit in the head by a discus while in high school, and also by a sledgehammer in a work accident. Several injuries also occurred as a result of beatings in his home. Radiological studies revealed lesions on his brain and a cyst as a result of childhood injuries. His mother felt that "maybe because he had been knocked unconscious a few times it distorted his thinking"—a bit of an understatement.

Environmental Trauma

Shawcross's history of trauma also fits the standard profile. He was seen as visibly unnerved in the presence of his mother. Once, during a visit with his parents while in prison, he just hung his head and spoke in baby talk. He always required mothering and nurturing from women, presumably to replace what he lacked from his mother.

His mother continuously berated him and disapproved of his actions. He never could please her or win her love in any way, nor could he develop any sense of esteem or intimacy. She constantly withheld physical and emotional love from Arthur, according to several reports, and treated him differently from than the "normal" children. She beat him regularly with a variety of instruments, yet she denied any deficiency in their relationship.

He spoke of an incident of oral sex with his sister, but reports of this incident remain inconsistent and are unsubstantiated. His experiences in Vietnam were also unsubstantiated, but appear to have had a profound effect on his life. He told stories of incredible violence, including:

I shot one woman and tied her up. . . . I cut the first girl's throat. Then I took off her head and placed it on a pole. The girl at the tree peed, then fainted. I gave her oral sex . . . then retied her to two other small trees. I cut her from neck to crotch. She screamed and shit herself . . . I took my M16, pulled on a nipple then put the gun to her forehead and pulled the trigger. Cut off her head and put it on a pole. . . . I killed 39 people in Vietnam. Scared alot and wounded more. When I left Vietnam, I wasn't ready for the states. (Olsen, 1993, pp. 190–91).

Early Antisocial Behavior and Prior Crimes

Along with his first murders and war crimes, Shawcross had a history of antisocial and illegal activity. He had a past filled with arson, theft, and breaking and entering, much of which he explained away as "not knowing what he was doing." He often blamed his actions on stressors such his divorce or alcohol.

However, his antisocial behaviors started at an early age. Arthur wet the bed and repeatedly ran away from home. A teacher reported that he brought an iron bar on the school bus and hit other children with it. He constantly was involved in fights and was ferociously brutal, as he never knew when to stop. He accompanied each blow with a sound effect from a comic book ("Bang!-Zap!-Pow!"). One school report stated "there is a general feeling one can't tell what he will do" (Olsen, 1993, p. 169).

Further evaluations noted that he had no playmates, was against everything at home, and directed hostility against defenseless objects and younger children. He would often talk baby talk and fake a cry to get attention. His scores in school were below normal, and he clearly demonstrated he did not care.

He still wet the bed in his teens and set fires, a behavior he began as a young child. He would often talk to himself in public, as others kept their distance. He also tortured animals regularly, and his cousin reported that he liked to watch them suffer and see how long it took them to die. Friends reported that this included skinning live fish, snaring rabbits and snapping their necks, placing bats inside parked cars to watch the drivers panic, tying cats together and drowning them, pounding squirrels and chipmunks flat, shooting darts at frogs nailed to his dart board, running a stick completely through a snapping turtle and scraping the feathers from baby birds.

His misbehavior continued, usually following his main interests of thievery, fire, and sex. Numerous scrapes with the law followed him straight to his draft into the army.

Problematic Sexual Deviance

Shawcross's sexual problems are also not hard to illustrate. In a statement he tried to explain how he was introduced to sex:

After I was first introduced to sex by my Aunt Tina, I became obsessed with sex . . . [he would constantly masturbate and have touching sessions with a another boy his age, about 9] . . . then I started to have oral sex with my sister. One time Mike [his friend] and I started playing with sheep. We didn't know that sheeps had organs like a woman. . . . When I was 14 a man gave me a ride, [then] grabbed me by the throat and told me to take my pants down. He held onto my balls and sucked me off. After that when I masturbated I could not cum until I inserted a finger in my ass. Why I don't know. One day I did it to a chicken. It died. Then a cow, a dog and a horse. I didn't know where this was leading up to. (Olsen, 1993, p. 184)

An army psychiatrist also warned Shawcross's wife to keep him away from fire, because arson provided him with sexual enjoyment. While in

Green Haven, the maximum-security correctional facility in Stormville, New York, where Arthur was imprisoned, he was often examined by psychiatrists and counselors. One diagnosis made there stated that he was a dangerous schizophrenic pedophile and had an oral-erotic fixation with need for maternal protection. Another referred to his psychosexual conflicts.

When his parole office referred Shawcross to the Genesee Mental Health Center, he was diagnosed as suffering from inhibited sexual excitement, inhibited orgasm, secondary impotence, sexual sadism, and a prostate ailment. He admitted to numerous (85–100) dates with prostitutes in Rochester, in an attempt to find out why he couldn't keep an erection or have an orgasm.

He killed some prostitutes after they mocked his sexual inadequacies. He also enjoyed having hookers "act dead" during sex, exciting him from a necrophilic standpoint of the total control and acceptance. He finally committed acts of cannibalism:

He returned to the site [of a prior murder where he buried the body in the snow] and with a small handsaw, scraped off the snow and cut out her vagina. "After I sawed it out, I pulled out the hairs and wrapped it in a bar towel. Went back to the car and . . . sat playing with myself and the vagina. Then I put it in my mouth and ate it. I had no control at all. Why did I do this?" (Norris, 1992, p. 47)

Dissociative Episodes

Shawcross reportedly showed periods of fantasy states and dissociation throughout his life. He commonly would "retreat into himself, mute and immobile for hours," according to his wife. Others spoke of his going for walks and blacking out, often not remembering where he'd been or what he'd done.

Diagnostic reports observed his hearing voices when depressed and the fact that he was "engaged in fantasy as a source of satisfaction." They also noted his inappropriate or lack of affect. A girlfriend also reported that he said he heard taunts in his head when he hid in the woods.

His childhood was colored with the same stories. A cousin noted that "Artie" always had a blank look, evident in baby pictures, looking straight ahead with no expression. At 7, he created imaginary friends out of loneliness. He carried on conversations at length, apparently talking to himself.

A teacher's evaluation said that he "appears to be indulging in a considerable amount of fantasy in which he perceives himself as a new person with respect and dignity" (Olsen, 1993, p. 170). Dr. Richard Kraus noted that Shawcross retreated to a fantasy world as a child, and thirty-five years and thirteen murders later was still involved in the same fantasies, "denying his failures and masculine inadequacy" (Olsen, 1993, p. 490).

Serial Murder

Arthur Shawcross meets the criteria for a serial killer. He, like many others, felt nothing toward his victims other than using them as sources of sexual satisfaction and stress relief. He killed children for sex and pleasure, spent seventeen years in prison, obtained his freedom, and promptly continued killing for his own gratification. He escalated as time went by, getting more careless and stepping up to cannibalism. He killed eleven more people and was stopped only through apprehension by law enforcement authorities.

Other Observations

Shawcross exhibited the impulse-control difficulties shown by many serial killers; he used anger to deal with stress. He also was seen to develop "elaborate and somewhat dysfunctional defenses in managing his feelings."

His past was filled with dysfunctional features, such as borderline personality disorder, schizophrenia, post-traumatic stress, anti social personality disorder, narcissism, sadism and psychopathic behavior. It also included long-term obsessive-compulsive behavior, prompting observations of Shawcross as someone evidencing an external attempt to control inner chaos. Also, returning to a scene and urinating over a recent victim in broad daylight is a classic way for the lust murderer to demonstrate control. It was during this important phase of behavior that he was observed and apprehended.

CASE 3: JEFFERY DAHMER

On Tuesday, July 23, 1991, Tracey Edwards, still wearing handcuffs, flagged down Milwaukee police and took them to Apartment 213 at 924 North 25th Street, where he said he had been the near-victim of a homicide.

Here, police discovered photographs of the mutilation of human bodies and the secret of Jeffery L. Dahmer was uncovered. Edwards, who later at trial said Dahmer had told him he would "eat his heart" (Witness, 1992), led police to where Dahmer had killed, dismembered, defiled, and even cannibalized a series of young men. This brought an end to a grisly pattern of death that had, for years, gone on seemingly unnoticed.

Dahmer's legacy began in 1979, when the then 18-year-old picked up a male hitchhiker and brought him to his grandmother's house for drinking and sex. When he attempted to leave, Dahmer hit him with a barbell, killing him. He then used a sledgehammer to smash the body into pieces and disposed of the evidence in nearby woods.

From that first murder until the time of his arrest, Dahmer admitted luring fifteen to seventeen men from various locations, including shopping malls, bus stops, and gay bars. He took them to his grandmother's house in West Allis, Wisconsin, and later to his apartment in Milwaukee, drugging and killing them.

He would offer his "guests" a concoction of alcohol or coffee, spiked with a sleeping potion suspected of being either a benzodiazepine such as Lorazepam (a tranquilizing medication he received while under treatment), menzodiazepine, or another undetected drug. Police also discovered chloroform in his closet (Davis, 1991, p. 275).

Dahmer admitted to taking pornographic and postmortem Polaroids of victims in various stages of mutilation, killing by strangulation, stabbing and battery, eviscerating the flesh, and dismembering the bodies. He told of cutting up the pieces with knives and an electric saw so they were small enough to be thrown in the trash or flushed down the toilet. He also melted down the torsos of victims in a fifty-seven-gallon drum of acid he kept in his apartment. He kept trophies, boiling the heads to keep the skulls and even painting them to make them appear artificial and more acceptable for display. He also kept body parts, such as skeletons, hands, and penises, for gratification and masturbation. (Milwaukee Police, 1991).

He subsequently admitted performing crude brain surgery on victims in hopes of creating zombies as sexual slaves. He told police he ate one victim's heart, a bicep, and a thigh, and planned to eat body parts stored in his refrigerator (Juror, 1992). He also had oral and anal sex with the bodies (Dvorchak and Holewa, 1991, p. 273). This necrophilia was introduced as evidence of an uncontrollable influence in his life by his defense, a cornerstone of his unsuccessful plea of insanity.

He was eventually found sane and guilty of fifteen counts of murder, receiving fifteen consecutive life sentences, totaling 962 years, before he would become eligible for parole. In his first public statement since the slayings, he told the judge he was not seeking freedom by pleading insanity, only understanding. "This has never been a case of trying to get free," he said (Dahmer, 1992). His prison stay was short, however, as he was beaten to death at Wisconsin's Columbia Correctional Center by another inmate in November 1994.

Physiological Factors

The majority of evidence regarding Dahmer's physiological abnormalities concerns his family history—mainly his father's childhood and his mother's condition prior to delivery. As a child, Jeffery Dahmer developed various infections that required injections. He also had a birth defect diagnosed as a double hernia. However, no other biological abnormalities were noted or, more specifically, measured in Dahmer himself. The biological factors regarding Dahmer appear inherited.

His mother, Joyce, experienced a litany of problems during her pregnancy, ranging from excessive nausea, extreme nervousness, severe depression, and hypersensitivity to noises and odors. She suffered from a lack of sleep and developed uncontrollable muscle spasms. About two months prior to Jeffery's birth, she developed a form of "rigidity," which her doctors could never precisely diagnose. She also suffered uncontrollable seizures:

At times, her legs would lock tightly in place, and her whole body would begin to tremble. Her jaw would jerk and take on a similarly frightening rigidity. During these strange seizures, her eyes would bulge like a frightened animal, and she would begin to salivate, literally frothing at the mouth. (Dahmer, 1994, pp. 33–34)

Joyce received a host of medications for her physical and emotional problems, including barbituates, morphine, and phenobarbital. Eventually, in the waning months of her pregnancy she was taking as many as twenty-six pills a day.

Dahmer's father, Lionel, had a childhood obsession with fires, one time almost burning down a neighbor's garage. Later, he began making bombs, once blowing a boy off a bicycle. He also noted a deep-rooted bond between himself and his son, in the sharing of recurring violent fantasies:

There were areas of my son's mind, tendencies and perversities which I had held within myself all my life. Jeff had multiplied these tendencies exponentially, his sexual perversion generating acts that were beyond my understanding. . . . Nonetheless, I could see their distant origins within myself, and slowly, over time, I began to see him truly as my son in far deeper ways than I had previously imagined. (Dahmer, 1994, p. 212)

Lionel Dahmer related observations of Jeff's violent thoughts and fantasies as a teenager, dreaming repeatedly of murder. He himself had shared these same fantasies and dreams from the age of 8 to his early twenties. He also recalled a desire as a child to hypnotize and control others, much like Jeffery's later cravings for "sex zombies."

Environmental Trauma

Dahmer's home life, while apparently not featuring physical abuse, was filled with upheaval and discontent. His parents' divorce was ugly, angry, and upsetting, and their bouts were legendary, including Joyce's threatening Lionel with a knife.

Jeff would flee the house during these brawls and slap at trees. An eventual custody battle ensued over his younger brother, David. His mother eventually abandoned Jeffery, alone in the house with little food, and left with David. He was 18 at the time, but not emotionally prepared for the situation. Jeff was found "shell-shocked and alone" like a "lost little boy" (Dahmer, 1994, p. 94). Also, found in the house was a pentagram drawn in chalk on an old coffee table. He admitted he was conducting a seance, trying to contact the dead.

Details of specific trauma are sketchy. After returning from prison (for child sexual assault) in 1990, he "had no light in his eyes. Jeff lost his soul in there. He said he'd never go back to prison," his stepmother Shari said. "Something happened to him in prison that he would never talk about. We all know what can happen to a child molester in prison" (Dvorchak & Holewa, 1991, p. 96).

An episode of the *Geraldo Rivera* TV show included a guest described as a former family acquaintance who called Shari "the epitome of the evil stepmother." This accusation, does not have much support from other accounts and is denied by family members, however.

Other accusations arose from that program. A man identified as "Nick," claiming to have had an extended homosexual relationship with Dahmer, said Jeff told him his father had sexually abused him. This was repeated on the *Phil Donahue* TV show, with the claim that the abuse lasted until Jeff was 16. Jeffery Dahmer immediately filed a legal affidavit denying he had ever been abused or molested by his father. His father also vehemently denied this. There were also vague reports about Dahmer's being molested as a child by some other individual in the neighborhood, but again details are unsubstantiated and unclear.

Early Antisocial Behavior and Prior Crimes

Dahmer was observed as never being able to converse with other children or relate to anyone. He almost invariably remained alone. His foolish acts in school had earned the label for anyone acting silly as "doing a Dahmer."

His first expression of violence was reported to have been an act of revenge. He gave a teaching assistant, for whom he developed a rare attachment, a bowl of tadpoles as a gift. She eventually gave the tadpoles to another child. Enraged, Dahmer snuck into the garage where they were kept and poured motor oil in the bowl, killing them.

At age 10, Dahmer was "experimenting" with dead animals, decapitating rodents, bleaching chicken and other animal bones with acid, nailing a dog's carcass to a tree and mounting its severed head on a stake (Newton, 1992, p. 103). He accumulated a vast collection of bodies in his animal cemetery and would impale the skulls of chipmunks and squirrels on crosses. His friends also noted that when they would go fishing, instead of tossing the catch back in the water Dahmer would cut it open, saying, "I want to see what it looks like inside" (Dvorchak and Holewa, 1991, pp. 40–41).

A pattern of antisocial and irresponsible behavior continued. He was caught with a friend stealing jewelry from his stepmother. In an attempt to get Jeff on the right course, his father enrolled him in a vocational school, only to find out from Jeff's grandmother that he had never attended the school.

His brushes with the law included public drunkenness, fights, an arrest for indecent exposure at a state fair, and for masturbating in public, witnessed by two 12-year-old boys. Later there was an arrest for drugging and sexually abusing a Laotian boy, who ended up being the brother of a future victim.

Problematic Sexual Deviance

Dahmer never had a meaningful sexual relationship with a woman. His homosexuality troubled him, becoming a problem as noted in the *DSM-IV* for a sexual disorder when one's sexual orientation leads to persistent and marked distress. It was the homosexuality factor that Dahmer saw in his victims.

His first killing apparently stemmed from an interlude with a male hitchhiker whose company he enjoyed. When the hitchhiker wanted to leave, Dahmer panicked. He crushed his skull and dismembered the body. He learned to associate violence with his need for intimacy with another man in order to avoid the thing he dreaded most—abandonment.

Dahmer claimed that he had interludes with over two hundred men he met cruising the gay bars and bathhouses of Milwaukee. The relationships were shallow, purely for sex, and devoid of meaningful aspects. His victims were male homosexuals, selected for their attractiveness and chosen to be his sex partners of unconditional acceptance. In other words, he wanted a hostage who could be directed to act as instructed, a warm torso where he could listen to body sounds, and eventually a corpse he could use for any form of personal gratification he chose.

When Dahmer spoke of fantasizing about attacking a jogger, it was in order to "lay with him." Dahmer's entire sexual motivation had developed into violence and ultimate demonstrations of control. Incredible thoughts of death and dismemberment had become sexually charged, driven, and satisfied. Dahmer also engaged in cannibalism, which was claimed to be a directly sexual act. Judith Becker, a defense expert witness, stated that "he would periodically take portions [of victims' remains] out of the freezer and cook them. When he ate them he would become sexually aroused" (Expert, 1992). There was no food in his apartment, only condiments. Inside the freezer were packed lungs, intestines, a kidney, a liver and a heart, he said "to eat later" (Chin and Tamarkin, 1991).

Dissociative Episodes

Jeffery Dahmer's body language suggested dissociation and his lack of affect was noted by family members as early as his childhood. "It was in his motionless face, his dull eyes, in the hard rigidity of his body, in the way his arms did not sway back and forth when he walked, even in the expressionless way he muttered 'sorry' " (Dahmer, 1994, p. 186). His stepmother, Shari, stated "he couldn't embrace. He couldn't touch. His eyes were dead. This child has no heart left within him. He was a walking zombie" (Dvorchak and Holewa, 1991, p. 32). His father continually referred to Jeff's demeanor as a "dull, unmoving mask" and noted he had "drifted into a nightmare world of unimaginable fantasies" and his "increasing inwardness and disconnection" (Dahmer, 1994, p. 81).

Dahmer would also drink himself into a numbed state, developing the alcoholism that eventually caused his discharge from the army.

Serial Murder

Dahmer's acts of predatorily killing at least fifteen men and performing sexual acts with the corpses qualifies him as a serial killer. He clearly understood the wrongness of his actions, but continued to fulfill the perverted desire to kill and defile the remains. His acts of cannibalism, trophy collection, ritual, and obsession with control are hallmarks of this diagnosis.

Other Observations

Some mental health professionals note that during Dahmer's killing career, he had a killing frenzy that represented reconnection with his estranged mother. There had been no contact for five years, then after a telephone call from her there was a spree of seven or eight murders. Dr. Ashok Bedi noted that the bulk of Dahmer's aggression took place after his mother's call. "It was almost as if he had finally managed to secure his mother's attention and he didn't want to lose it again. By doing what he has done, he has irreversibly connected their fates" (Davis, 1991, p. 262).

CASE 4: EDMUND KEMPER

Edmund Kemper set a chilling example for those who would attempt the risky practice of predicting dangerousness. He was incarcerated for the double homicide of his grandparents at age 15. He was "deemed cured in 1969, and the California Youth Authority, responsible for juvenile offenders, took charge of him for the next three years. He was freed in 1972" (Ellroy, 1991, p. 165). Similar to Arthur Shawcross, Kemper proceeded to commit the grisly murders of eight women, soon after his ill-fated release, decapitating and cannibalizing some of them and performing sexual acts with the corpses.

He was raised by a "shrilly belittling university administrator (and her succession of husbands, none of whom could measure up to her fierce social ambitions) who locked him in a cellar and endlessly berated him for his social failures" (Leyton, 1986, p. 25).

Kemper, who displayed repeated incidences of sadistic behavior as a child, was sent to live with his grandparents. After an argument with his grandmother in August of 1963, he shot her in the back of the head with a rifle, then stabbed her repeatedly after she was dead. He then shot his grandfather and subsequently called the sheriff to confess. He reportedly said during the confession, "I just wondered how it would feel to shoot Grandma" (Cheney, 1992, p. 22).

The doctors recommended, after five years at Atascadero State Hospital, above all that he never be returned to live with his mother. The Youth Authority kept him for three months, then promptly returned him to his mother. Kemper's difficult relationship with his mother only worsened, escalating into furious fights as she ridiculed and embarrassed him. He soon began rehearsing his plans for murder while picking up an estimated 150 hitchhikers in 1970–1971, then finally committed the first of his serial murders.

He killed two coed hitchhikers in May 1972, took the corpses home, and cut them up while his mother was out. He buried the remains in the mountains. He continued killing hitchhikers, carving them up and performing sexual acts with the cadavers. Once his mother was at home, causing him to have to wait until the next day to dissect and have sex with two of the bodies. Another time, he sliced flesh from the legs of at least two bodies and ate it in a macaroni casserole as a way of "possessing" his victims.

Eventually, Kemper realized the most prominent of his murderous fantasies. As a child he would periodically slip into his mother's room with a hammer and knife and fantasize about killing her. Now, faced with the impending discovery of evidence that might tie him to one of the murders, he decided it was time to kill his mother:

Once she had fallen asleep, at five in the morning, Kemper took a claw hammer from the kitchen and, as he had done so often in his imagination, went into her bedroom while she slept. This time, he actually brought the hammer down with considerable force on her right temple, then slashed her throat with his pocketknife. Blood was still gushing as he decided to sever the head as he had done with his other victims. Another slice removed her larynx, and he threw this part into the disposal unit in the kitchen sink. When the disposal was unable to digest the larynx and spewed it back out, Kemper thought this was poetic justice. He wrapped the body in bloody sheets and stashed it in the closet. (Ressler, 1992, pp. 257–58)

Kemper raped the headless corpse of his mother and propped the head on the mantle for use as a dart board. Not yet satisfied, he invited a friend of his mother over for a surprise dinner in his mother's honor. He bludgeoned and strangled her, decapitated the corpse, and left the headless body in his bed.

After a brief flight, he called authorities and confessed to eight murders. When asked what he thought his punishment should be, he replied, "death by torture." He received life in prison with the possibility of parole.

Physiological Factors

Physiological research regarding Kemper is incomplete. During some interviews, it has been reported that he would have fits, wobbling his head while never changing the position of his arms, and fixing a gaze on the interviewer. His face would become flushed, his breath came quickly, and he would begin to stutter (Cheney, 1992, p. 195). Kemper also reported experiencing hallucinations and referred to losing control of his body during the killing of his grandparents. His episodes of mental involuntary seizures were what he called his "little zapples."

No organic brain disease was reported during the trial phase. It is not clear what sort of testing, or to what extent, was administered. Kemper, after sentencing, also requested psychosurgery to control his violence and to become productive again. Psychiatrist David Lunde dismissed any application of the XYY theory to Kemper, although he noted that Edmund fit the description of the XYY—unusually tall, above-average intelligence, and unusually violent (Leyton, 1986, p. 59). However, it is unclear what type of testing was done or, more importantly, was not done.

Finally, consideration must be given to Kemper's unusual and enormous size, "in 1969, a 21-year-old behemoth grown to six-foot-nine and some 300 pounds" (Newton, 1990, p. 180).

Environmental Trauma

Kemper's environment was the most obvious dimension of his development. The product of a broken and abusive home, he was belittled by a shrewish mother, who occasionally locked him in the basement when he failed to meet her standards of behavior. He grew up timid and resentful, nursing a perception of his own inadequacy that gave rise to morbid fantasies of death and mutilation (Newton, 1990, p. 179). He was eventually banished to the basement, as his enormous size made his sisters uncomfortable and his mother considered him a sexual threat to them. His hellish relationship with his mother destroyed any possible sense of esteem, and ended in her murder. His home was replete with "an alcoholic and overbearing mother, an absent father, favored sisters and a grandmother who was in many ways a worse nurturer than the mother" (Ressler, 1992, p. 249). His mother continuously belittled and embarrassed him, and told him he was the source of her problems. She remarried and divorced twice more between the time Kemper was 10 and 14. Each time, when the marriage was going badly, he would be sent to live with his grandparents on their farm. He hated that and eventually killed them both.

His mother continued to blame her dating problems on Edmund. She once told him, "because of you, my murderous son, I haven't had sex with a man for five years, because no one wants to be with me out of fear of you." She never stopped abusing him mentally (Ressler, 1992, p. 250). He said that their relationship was filled with continuous verbal warfare, so vicious that they would have resulted in fistfights had they not involved his mother. He felt she "insisted" on these battles, usually over insignificant topics such as having his teeth cleaned (Cheney, 1992, pp. 37–38).

Although the mental health professionals at Atascadaro recognized the incredibly negative effect she had on his obviously fragile psyche, and despite the fact they that strenuously objected to releasing him in her custody, the courts did just that.

Early Antisocial Behavior and Prior Crimes

Edmund's violent nature was evident from the beginning. As a child, he often played a game in which his sisters took the part of executioners, with Kemper as their victim, writhing in imaginary death throes when they "threw the switch." Preoccupied with visions of decapitation and dismemberment, he cut off the head and hands of his sister's doll—a modus operandi he would repeat as an adult with humans (Newton, 1990, p. 179).

Before the age of 10, he killed his first cat—to make it his—by burying it alive in the yard. When it was dead, he brought it into the house and cut off its head, which he stuck on a spindle and kept in his room. He prayed over it (Cheney, 1992, p. 9).

He later shot to death a pet dog belonging to another boy in the neighborhood. At 13, he was sharpening his father's machete while sitting in the same room with the family's Siamese cat. The pet sometimes seemed to ignore him and appeared to prefer his sisters (much like his mother). Suddenly,

without even feeling angry toward the cat, he picked it up by the nape of the neck, seized the machete, and slashed off the top of the cat's skull, noting with surgical interest that he had thus exposed the brain. The cat went into convulsions. Edmund, splattered with blood, seized a knife and, holding the cat by one of the forelegs, proceeded to stab it repeatedly in the chest and abdomen. . . . Fearing his mother would call the police and have him jailed, he picked up the dead animal, buried it in the backyard, and cleaned up the mess in his room. Parts of the cat, for reasons that he did not fully understand, he decided to hide in his closet. (Cheney, 1992, p. 15)

Problematic Sexual Deviance

Kemper's assessment of his sexual past was that it was poor, although the particular stories vary. He reported he had a normal sexual relationship only once, but also said that on other occasions he never did and again that he frequently attempted intercourse but never reached climax. He admittedly was constantly consumed with thoughts of sex. In any case, his sexual history was clearly abnormal.

One afternoon, at 7 years old, he was discussing a childish crush on a teacher. His sister asked why he didn't just kiss her. His deadly serious response was, "If I kiss her, I would have to kill her first." His entire childhood was full of violent fantasy attached to sexual urges. Identified by mental health professionals as a classic sadist, his entire sexual orientation was based on carnage and necrophilia, as well as on the sexual implications of his cannibalism.

His sexual drive conflicted with his incapacities. His earliest sexual fantasies were of women, but the key area was not orgasm but the fact the woman was dead. He felt inadequate sexually, and therefore sexual fantasies were primarily dissatisfying. He said, "I couldn't follow through on the male end of the responsibility, so . . . if I killed them, they couldn't reject me as a man. It was more or less making a doll out of human being" (Leyton, 1986, p. 41).

He had repeated sexual fantasies about his mother and sisters, also complete with violence. He once stood outside a teacher's house one night and imagined what it would be like to kill her and make love to her. He also imagined what it would be like to kill his neighbors and have sex with the corpses (Martingale, 1993, pp. 86–87).

Kemper's need for violence was clear in his having very little sexual contact until after he killed. Moreover, the only act he found sexually exciting was decapitation:

I remember there was actually a sexual thrill, he said, for he loved to hear the "pop" when the head was separated from the body. You hear that little pop and pull their heads off and hold their heads up by the hair. Whipping their heads off, their body sitting there. That'd get me off. (Leyton, 1986, p. 42)

Dissociative Episodes

Kemper's fantasies have been related often in this study. Escaping from his terrible family life and left with no playmates or friends, he escaped to his mind, filled with violent and sexual fantasy. This was his place of comfort.

In his fantasies, the person was depersonalized, made into an object. "I'm sorry to sound so cold about this," Kemper said, "but what I needed to have was a particular experience with a person, and to possess them in the way I wanted to; I had to evict them from their human bodies." In other words, Kemper was saying that in order to have his sexual fantasies fulfilled, he had to kill his partner (Ressler, 1992, p. 97).

He often sat and stared at people until he made them uncomfortable, in dissociative-like states. In a statement sounding like someone experiencing a mental state resembling dissociation, he once stated, "I believe . . . that there are two people inside me." At times it seemed to him the killings were "horrendous," yet at other times he said "those feelings don't enter my mind" (Cheney, 1992, p. 171).

Serial Murder

Edmund Kemper killed a total of ten people; however, not including the killing of his grandparents at age 15, only the eight committed after his release from Atascadaro are considered serial. He did stalk and kill the victims in an obsessive fashion, and he cannibalized and sexually defiled them. He kept trophies and escalated into a frenzy toward the end of his rampage. He fits the criteria of a serial killer.

Other Observations

It is interesting to note a psychiatrist's observation of Kemper, who during the trial, seemed to get great satisfaction and enjoyment from his new-found status as a highly publicized killer. It was suggested that this was the recognition sorely lacking and so craved in his childhood (Cheney, 1992, p. 181). This, of course, is not uncommon among serial killers and is consistent with their narcissistic and overcompensating nature.

He also displayed the obsessive-compulsive pattern of escalation reminiscent of many serial murderers. Kemper mentioned that late in his homicidal career, the urge to kill again struck him as often as a week or two after his last murder. He said the urge was powerful and "the longer I let it go, the stronger it got, to where I was taking risks to go out and kill people" (Cheney, 1992, p. 140).

6

Case Studies Analysis

I wasn't going to rob her, or touch her, or rape her. I just wanted to kill her.
—David Berkowitz

METHODOLOGY

As stated earlier, these cases were selected mainly for their relative completeness and the fact that they cover a workable time span. This is not to say the information on the subjects is be truly complete, especially in the older cases, but every effort was made to maximize the scope of information.

Information sources included books, newspapers, magazines and journals, film, television, police reports, interviews, personal communication, and other case materials. It would have been best to offer a true triangulation of data by complementing the written data with personal interviews, but unfortunately requests for interviews were denied by Dahmer before his death and the chances of obtaining time with the surviving men appear remote.

In accumulating the data, a system of recording the measurable elements was applied, these elements generated by the significant factors discussed in Chapter 4: evidence of biological conditions, environmental trauma, early crimes, dissociation, and sexual dysfunction.

Examination of the case histories of Chikatilo, Shawcross, Dahmer, and Kemper reveals details of their pasts that are truly relevant to this analysis and suggest certain patterns, discussed here. Overall interpretation and discussion is held until Chapters 7 and 8.

Evidence of Physiological Factors

The appearance of physical abnormalities in these case studies was consistent, although difficult to measure. Andrei Chikatilo's youth revealed different instances of head trauma. There was also a diagnosis of dystonia. During the murder investigation, it was revealed he had a rare combination of blood and semen type. There were reports of severe headaches throughout his history, an affliction his mother reportedly shared.

Arthur Shawcross's case history, contained the most solid evidence of various physiological anomalies. The extensive evidence of abnormalities included elevated kryptopyrrole levels, abnormal EEGs, and XYY genetic coding. Reports also included stories of repeated head injuries and other physical traumas.

Points of interest within Jeffery Dahmer's physical history most often concerned his parents. There was familial evidence of excessive prenatal medication by his birth mother, plus she experienced seizures. Also, there was reported paternal obsession with fire and violence from early ages.

Edmund Kemper's physical history and background were the least complete of the group. Very little formal analysis was done, as compared to the Shawcross case. There were reported fits and seizures by Kemper, but no organic brain disease was noted.

The biological aspects of this study are the most incomplete for this study. It is not customary to run a complete battery of physiological tests on convicted murderers as was done in the case of Shawcross, therefore many potential results are not available.

Some evidence of personal biological abnormality is clear for Shawcross, or for in the family in Dahmer's case, but physical histories are not as complete for the other two subjects. This is especially true of Chikatilo, as these analyses were unheard of in Russia at the time.

That information is limited for Chikatilo and Kemper, however, does not mean that biological abnormalities were not present. It simply means that the possibility of including such data does not exist.

Evidence of Environmental Trauma

The history of Andrei Chikatilo is highlighted by extensive poverty and famine, as well as exposure to grotesque physical injuries. He also believed a story regarding his brother's capture and cannibalization, although this is difficult to confirm. He had no father or friends as a child, and was socially ostracized by those in his village when he was a youth.

Various physical and mental abuses filled Arthur Shawcross's childhood. His tortuous relationship with his mother was damaging and lifelong, while his father played a weak role. He also had no friends as a child, owing to his extremely low socioeconomic status and frightening personality. There were also reports of possible sexual abuse.

Jeffery Dahmer's chaotic and disturbing home life was intensified by his parents' bitter divorce, which came at a time when he appeared most emotionally vulnerable. He was abandoned by his mother at a time when he found loneliness to be devastating. He also did not enjoy the company of friends as a child. Again, there were reports of possible sexual abuse.

Edmund Kemper's alcoholic and mentally abusive mother rivaled Shawcross's in pure dysfunction. His grandmother was not any better, he did not have a father, and his sisters were physically afraid of him. His history includes tales of physical abuse. As were the other subjects, he was rejected by siblings and peers.

A dysfunctional environment is a trait shared by all the killers in the study. Problems ranging from chaotic home lives to physical and mental abuse existed. All the subjects had childhoods that could be viewed, at the very least, as excessively difficult, and most likely damaging and traumatic.

All subjects clearly had serious obstacles in their ability to develop a reasonable sense of self, normal attachments, or strong positive role models, as well as little chance to understand intimacy or sexuality.

Observation of Prior Criminality

Prior criminality is one of the easier items to identify in these case studies. Andrei Chikatilo built an extensive career as a child molester and sadist, seeking employment to facilitate exposure to children and potential victims. His past also suggests the possibility of incidences of burglary.

Arthur Shawcross's records reveal incidences of arson, burglary, and extreme violence toward others, beginning at a very early age. He suffered from late bed-wetting and engaged in continued torture of animals. He enjoyed an extensive history of sexual misconduct and child molestation.

Jeffery Dahmer's past was full of early antisocial behavior and problems in school. He, too, engaged in continued animal abuse. Later on, he experienced employment difficulties and repeated bouts with alcoholism. He had scrapes with the law involving child molestation as well as burglary.

Edmund Kemper displayed an early obsession with violence, death, and sadism, disturbing everyone who viewed it. He practiced extreme animal abuse and had a long pattern of sexual misconduct. He was institutionalized for the double homicide of his grandparents at age 15.

All four subjects share a degree of early criminality and antisocial behavior, ranging from burglary to extreme violence and sexual offenses. These individuals displayed markedly noticeable antisocial behaviors that should have alerted the people close to them. They were clearly not just immature, working through the typical personality problems of development.

The evidence of crimes involving fire setting and extreme animal abuse suggests that biological factors include lack of impulse control and a predisposition to violence. Other crimes, such as burglary, may involve a seizing of control, possibly on a sexual level.

Incidence of Sexual Dysfunction

Sexual dysfunction is a factor that is not difficult to observe. Andrei Chikatilo was an extreme sexual sadist, pedophile, and child molester. He continuously struggled to attain erection and orgasm, later developing a penchant for necrophilia and cannibalism.

Arthur Shawcross's entire life revolved around various sexual dysfunctions and perversions. He was sexually charged by arson and violence. Similar to the other subjects, he encountered erection and orgasmic difficulties. Beastiality, sexual sadism, necrophilia, child molestation, and cannibalism were in his paraphilic portfolio.

Jeffery Dahmer dealt with a long-term conflict within himself concerning his homosexuality. He had no "normal" sexual relationships in his personal history, neither heterosexual nor homosexual. He engaged in exhibitionism, child molestation, and necrophilia as well as cannibalism.

Edmund Kemper's personality was dominated by his extreme sexual sadism and interest in masochism. He was also obsessed with necrophilia and, as found in the other three subjects, cannibalism. The subjects' various extreme sexual dysfunctions are the most obvious aspect of this study. None of these case histories show any "normal" (or at least not dysfunctional) sexual patterns or relationships. Conversely, not only did they share problematic feelings of inferiority and difficulty or anxiety regarding performance (as does much of the population), they all engaged in extremely dangerous and threatening sexual activity. Violence and death were pervasive themes. It is also interesting to note that all subjects were reported to have engaged in necrophilia and cannibalism, suggesting ultimate issues of power and control fused with sexuality.

Observation of Fantasy and Dissociation

Andrei Chikatilo was often observed in a continued fantasy state. There were repeated public incidences of emotional detachment. Arthur Shawcross's family and acquaintances reported that he engaged in fantasy-obsessed behavior throughout his life, and was often observed in lengthy periods of dissociation.

Jeffery Dahmer, too, displayed a lifelong lack of affect and was observed in deep fantasy states. Everyone in his immediate family reported his states of dissociation. Finally, Edmund Kemper's history revealed a pattern of deep fantasy states and that he had trancelike episodes.

All of the case histories show how the subjects spent extended periods of time in fantasy or dissociative states. These episodes would often be observed in public, including at work or in school, not only while the subject could be considered "alone with his thoughts."

The subjects displayed these traits from a very early age, possibly compensating for a lack of social contact and withdrawing to a safe place within their own minds.

Serial Murderer: An Appropriate Diagnosis?

It is clear from this analysis that there is a consistent pattern for this criminal. All killed in a predatory manner, deriving satisfaction (or relief) from the very act of killing. They continued their activities regardless of the obvious wrongfulness and potential consequences, while remaining aware to avoid detection. They killed in an obsessive, cyclical fashion, exhibiting a period of anxiety before killing and displaying a time break between victims, commonly referred to as a cooling-off period (Ressler et al., 1984).

This pattern constitutes a set of consistent activities that can be diagnosed and categorized, as noted by Apsche (1993). The behaviors and etiology are found across the board, and are discussed at length in Chapter 8.

SUMMARY: POSITIVE AND NEGATIVE ASSUMPTIONS

The negative observations in this limited study simply do not exist. The weakest factors are the biological ones and even they do offer some support for the theory proposed here. Again, this weakness is due to the lack of available testing, perhaps showing an apparent bias by researchers against biological factors.

Regarding the other factors in this study—namely, Was there environmental trauma? Were there prior crimes? Was there sexual dysfunction? Were there dissociative episodes? Is there a recognizable syndrome called a serial murderer?—the answers must be a resounding yes. There is no question that these factors and patterns were present, and they cannot be explained away by differences in interpretation.

7

Theoretical Analysis and Development

I think I got more of a high out of killing than molesting.

—Westley Alan Dodd

Any reflection on these case histories makes, revision of initial impressions a necessity. The analysis, in conjunction with the patterns found in the literature review, drive the following conclusions and result in a comprehensive theory regarding the development of serial killers.

In this chapter, the resulting theory is broken down into three separate stages: (1) the foundation, or primal basis of the pathology; (2) the path of the stressors, which combine with predisposition as they develop to the first murder; and (3) the obsessive-compulsive and ritualistic cycle of serial murder. Each component of each stage is briefly reviewed here, as they have been discussed at length in earlier chapters.

STAGE 1: FOUNDATION OF PATHOLOGY

Figure 7.1 shows the basic ingredients and combination of factors that lead to the development of the serial killer.

Figure 7.1
Foundation of Pathology

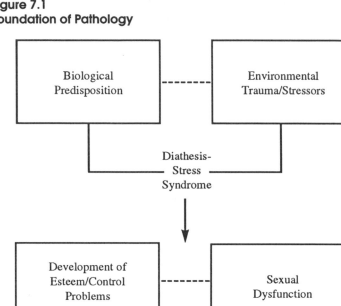

Biological Predisposition

A biological predisposition, as examined in the literature review, remains a critical point of this theory. Biological abnormality appears consistently in the case histories discussed, and although its presence remains basically intuitive and correlational, it combines with environmental trauma to produce the dynamic for the diathesis-stress model. Environment alone does not appear to produce the serial killer, so it seems the biological factor is key to the mix.

Environmental Trauma and Stressors

The catalyst of the diathesis-stress model is the environmental trauma shared by all the subjects of these case histories, as well as the vast majority of other serial killers. Clearly, there is no dispute regarding the trauma these killers sustained, for both the cases reviewed here and those outside the scope of this analysis. A history of environmental trauma is shared by all so this factor constitutes the second half of the diathesis-stress theory.

Development of Esteem and Control Problems

The case histories reveal the direct result of traumas experienced in childhood that resulted in a disastrous loss of self-esteem, a lack of sense of self, and thwarted development of a sense of intimacy. The personality problems of Chikatilo, Shawcross, Dahmer, and Kemper all progressed to greater degrees as they grew older.

Socioeconomic factors combined with familial failures to rob these subjects of a fair chance at personality development. This feature was found in all the case histories, usually interacting with their traumatic backgrounds and decidedly damaging their personalities during critical stages of formation.

Sexual Dysfunction

Sexual problems go hand-in-hand with personality problems and serve as a springboard for life in a fantasy world, obsessive behavior, criminal activity, and sexually dysfunctional preferences and motivations.

Sexual difficulties are a prevalent aspect of these offenders' lives and serve as a bridge, taking the killers from early stages of inadequacy, anger, and frustration to worlds of seeking out deviant sex featuring control, dominance, and dangerous paraphilia.

STAGE 2: PATH OF STRESSORS AND DEVELOPMENT TO FIRST MURDER

Development of Maladaptive Coping Skills

The poor personality traits (low self-esteem, lack of sense of self) and coping skills demonstrated by these subjects resulted in their maladaptive reactions to society. All of the subjects withdrew into private worlds and expressed their frustrations by committing crimes even before their serial murder careers began.

These individuals, both the subjects of the case histories and other killers mentioned in the literature, never learned to truly relate to others in their families or society, providing a basis for troubles to come. These maladaptive coping mechanisms determined how the subjects dealt with family, friends, potential lovers, and anyone else with whom they interacted. Difficulties with sex, personal relationships, and friendships of any quality, as well as problems with day-to-day interactions with people were inevitable.

Retreat into Fantasy World

A consistent maladaptive coping process among these subjects was their total withdrawal into fantasy worlds. Not only could they escape to these private worlds and enjoy their unacceptable sexual preferences, but they could also change their surroundings entirely. They found acceptance, status, and the other missing parts of their lives in these fantasy worlds.

Retreat into fantasy, as discussed in previous chapters, is endlessly attractive. Eliminating other people and their impossible standards eradicates the enormous stress and certain failure these killers anticipate in their interactions with others. This is not to say that fantasy in itself can drive homicidal patterns of behavior; fantasy is enjoyed by a large segment of the population without dire consequences. It is just that a combination of a maladaptive personality and a fantasy life allow deviant sexual themes and violent ideas to become reality for the developing serial killer personality.

Lesser Crimes

The manifestations of poor coping skills are often criminal behaviors, in both an antisocial disregard for authority and attempts to secure control and status. As shown in Figure 7.2, the maladaptive coping skills progress to criminality and disregard for others.

Some behaviors manifested in the case histories were fetish burglaries or other sexually charged attempts at seizing control. Sexual misconduct with children or other powerless subjects also demonstrates a consistent goal of achieving the control and acceptance missing from these subjects' lives.

Disastrously developed sexual dysfunctions such as pedophilia, necrophilia, and sexual sadism as evidenced in the case studies, also results in criminal activity and forced violence.

Figure 7.2
Path of Stressors Leading to First Murder

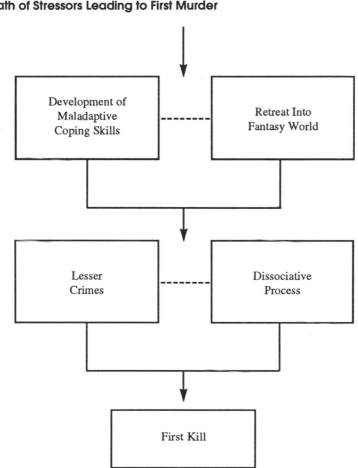

Dissociative Process

The dissociative process, which appears to be a higher state of fantasy, is the next level to which the fledgling serial killers move, by drawing real people into their dark fantasy worlds. As analysis of the case studies shows, there is a key difference between fantasy and dissociation.

It is one thing to be continuously lost in a dream world of fantasies, consciously creating an arena of unconditional love and acceptance, as well as sexual satisfaction. However, in a dissociative state, the subject takes this mental orientation to its moral and legal limits and advances toward a physical realization of his spiritual cravings.

The developing killer is often lost in a fantasy state, and returns there to enjoy the crimes again and again. However, the dissociative process begins when a Chikatilo becomes a wild beast, a Shawcross sees someone else kill, a serene Dahmer face becomes a mask of evil, and a Kemper lives out his childhood rehearsal for murder. It is a doubling process that allows the individual to fulfill his deadly compulsion.

First Kill

Eventually the offender loses control of a situation—during a child rape (Chikatilo, Shawcross), when he feels panic or fear of another rejection (Dahmer), or in an explosive rage (Kemper). The trigger may have been a significant stressful event. Whatever, the situation is perceived of and reacted to in a way far different from that of an average citizen. The killer reaches a breaking point and, at last, commits his first homicide. The act is inevitable, and it introduces the killer to an obsessive cycle from which he can never escape.

STAGE 3: OBSESSIVE-COMPULSIVE AND RITUALISTIC CYCLE

Renewed Urge to Kill

The killer has begun the cycle (Figure 7.3). Chikatilo now knows what he needs for sexual gratification. Dahmer now knows he must continually murder for men to lay with. Kemper knows he will kill his mother again and again until he gets it right, reveling in the sheer sadism of his action. Shawcross knows he must cruise for prostitutes until one strikes him just right, to pay for his rejection by and hatred for women.

The killer has experienced the act that will now become his addiction. He has a taste for blood that cannot be satisfied by anything less.

Figure 7.3
Obsessive-Compulsive Ritualistic Cycle

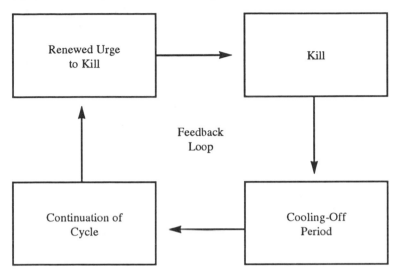

Cooling-off Period

A central portion of the cycle is the cooling off, or the period between murders. There may be shame, or fear of detection and reprisal. However, Chikatilo waits until the weather and time is right to again satisfy his thirst. Kemper and Shawcross try to control themselves, but fail. Dahmer allows potential victims to leave because they are not his type or he doesn't have enough time before work, but eventually he caves in to his compulsion.

Another aspect of this cooling-off period is the reliving of the crime. The mental rush and sexual thrill is renewed when these deeds are replayed. the mental repetition reinforces the behavior and ensures the inevitable reoccurrence of the crime.

Continuation of Cycle

The cycle repeats itself. In the cases on Andrei Chikatilo, Arthur Shawcross, Jeffery Dahmer, and Edmund Kemper, the killers were doomed to cyclical patterns of murder, cooling off, renewed urge, and murder. They became ritualistic, addicted to their patterns of death and achieving orgasm, collect trophies, and avoiding detection. The tension before the act and the relief afterwards cements the pattern. The cycle escalates until an eventual overkill or gap in security dooms the killers to discovery.

These wretched souls, as well as countless others, have joined the ranks of serial murderers, a pathological obsession that possibly only the most extreme alcoholics and drug addicts might understand.

8

Conclusion

You feel the last bit of breath leaving their body. You're looking into their
eyes. A person in that situation is God. You possess them and they shall
forever be a part of you.

—Ted Bundy

A CRITICAL LOOK AT THIS ANALYSIS

A weakness that stands out in this study is the lack of detail concerning
biological factors. There is an inconsistency to the data available, mainly
owing to the patchwork design of testing. If a greater proportion of
offenders were given the extensive biological analysis that Shawcross
received, rather than the minimal consideration Chikatilo was given, this
dimension could be either strengthened or disputed.

The inadequacy of data here reduces the biological component to one
of intuition, based on the correlational nature of the research. This study
would be strengthened with greater quantitative credibility for biological
determinants.

Another weakness is anecdotal nature of case studies. However, as
previously discussed, this type of research is most appropriate for limited
samples such as this. The actual statistical data are limited and difficult to

extract, so the case study approach allows for a look at the complete picture.

It should be noted that the case study method does weed out inconsistencies during its accumulation of facts. For example, it has been questioned whether Jeffery Dahmer actually committed cannibalism during his active period. A look at other serial killers shows that they did commit cannibalism, most notable Des Nilsen, a killer often paralleled with Dahmer. Admittedly, it is possible that all these subjects are lying and/or embellishing, but as more reports accumulate, this becomes less likely.

Does consistency of reports prove unequivocally that cannibalism occurred? No, but the possibility appears much more likely, given the circumstances. This is especially true when viewed in the context of the control and acceptance issues that the act of cannibalism implies.

Issues for Future Analysis

The aspect of control is a topic needing further development. Issues of control are pervasive and consistent, but a closer look at this dimension has merit. For example, control-related behaviors during the offenses might be identified and examined. Similar backgrounds could also be considered.

It also would be interesting to see a more extensive analysis of prior criminality. Many of the crimes—breaking and entering, burglary, exhibitionism, arson—have a sexual or control drive element to them. Robert Ressler often refers to "fetish burglaries," or crimes committed in the acting-out motivation regarding control and sexual issues. This type of crime, with all its implications, would make a worthwhile study.

Regarding biological factors, recent studies linking serotonin levels, impulsive violence, and suicide suggest possible analyses of suicidal behavior or ideation in serial killers. Additionally, studies continue to report correlations between genetics and behavior. Dopamine effects on thrill seeking and excitability (Studies find, 1996), as well as the effects of nitric oxide on violent and sexually aggressive behavior (Toufexis, 1995) have been cited. These findings and others point to a need for exploration of the biological arena. Neurological studies, consideration of infections, genetic analyses, and even brain examinations after death, as have been suggested regarding John Wayne Gacy and Jeffery Dahmer, would likely offer additional insight into this issue.

Methodological Changes

The most important methodological change or improvement to this analysis would be in the realm of biological study. Ideally, each subject would receive a complete work-up similar to that done for Arthur Shawcross. This is unlikely, however performing standardized measures of key elements such as kryptopyrrole levels or other genetic markers on more offenders would be beneficial.

Another possibility is to analyze in detail exactly what points might best characterize a biological predisposition. Certain particulars, such as kryptopyrrole levels, brain trauma, or heredity, might be examined or measured for consistency among offenders. Along the same lines, those specific behaviors discussed in this book, such as prior crimes or dissociative episodes, could be narrowed and analyzed as separate studies.

Additional Case Testing

Additional case studies could extend this theory to include types of serial killers, such as females or those with a venue outside the US other than Chikatilo. A study concerning female killers would likely be of great interest, by examining the similarities and differences with male counterparts—the matter of biological influence could be a key issue. Another study could categorize killers by type of victims, similar background, or time period.

A study similar to this one could be constructed using a larger selection of case histories. Given the extensive literary review necessary to formulate this preliminary model, more than four cases would have been unworkable. However, if another study replicated and measured the theory suggested here, the majority of time and effort could be spent on obtaining larger sample.

Protocols for Validation through Interviews

In-depth, complete interviews would be an excellent way to further validate this study. The data would be less second-hand and anecdotal, and interpretation would be consistent. The interviews would necessarily include:

1. Investigation of biological factors
2. Questions regarding fantasies

3. Questions regarding the sexual nature of early crimes
4. Inquiry into sexual problems and proclivities
5. Complete examination of the environmental situation
6. Examination of clinical psychological background
7. Discussion of an obsessive or cyclical pattern of crimes

Structure would be the key component of the interview. It would be necessary to conduct repeated interviews, not too long as to cause the subject to lose interest, but not too short as to ensure the subject has opportunity to free-think verbally. Repetition is necessary to weed out possible embellishments and lies, and to establish consistent stories and histories.

It would also be advantageous to interview family and acquaintances. Former teachers, psychologists, and employers would provide an interesting dimension. The interviews should, however, be conducted by the same interviewer to ensure continuity. However, a key element would be careful standardization of data to allow inference across cases.

CONCLUSIONS AND DISCUSSION

It would be unrealistic to assume that the model suggested in this book is all-inclusive; even the FBI's Behavioral Sciences Unit assumes its rules of profiling to be applicable in about 75 percent of situations (Ressler, 1992, p. 129). Often, profiling attempts during investigations are revised according to additional data as it is received. This, along with the considerable overlap of many "organized" and "disorganized" offenders, and individual variables, makes it difficult to generalize.

Dispute may rage as to the relative weight of factors such as biology, trauma, and sexual deviance. In some cases, biological predisposition has a greater impact; in others, environment plays a larger role. Some may suggest that pornography, pressures from society, or other factors are virtually ignored in this particular study. However, the dynamics suggested in this model are consistent and difficult to deny.

Most, if not all, serial killers display some evidence of the psychological syndromes discussed. Common factors include questionable genetics and biology, as well as emotional problems concerning sense of self and control. There may be questions regarding the relative weights in each case, but both biological and traumatic factors seem to exist in the majority of serial killers, whereas the presence of either one or the other does not.

Sexual dysfunction and deviance are pervasive themes, as is the link between mental and physical influences. Finally, the obsessive-compulsive cycle of serial murders is well documented.

The focal points in this proposal center on circulated about two issues: (1) the serial murderer as a diagnosable syndrome that should be clinically recognized, and (2) a theory of violence based on the diathesis-stress model, with identifying features as applied to the serial killer.

The Syndrome of Serial Murder

Robert Ressler once asked Edmund Kemper where he thought he would fit in the *Diagnostic and Statistical Manual of Mental Disorders*. He replied that he didn't find a description that fit him, and didn't expect to until psychiatry had obtained sufficient information to understand people like him. He felt this might be by the sixth or seventh edition, probably some time in the next century (Ressler, 1992, p. 248).

The analysis of the cases in this study, along with the literature review, suggests very strongly that there is a clustering of behaviors and traits consistent enough to be recognized and categorized in a diagnostic manual such as the *Diagnostic and Statistical Manual of Mental Disorders* (American Psychiatric Association, 1994). The serial murderer displays a pattern of behavior no less diagnosable than the antisocial or borderline personalities, or someone suffering from post-traumatic stress syndrome.

This position in no way suggests that an offender diagnosed thus so is deserving of exculpatory status; in fact, quite the opposite. Insanity, as is well known, is but a legal distinction. It usually refers to a person's ability to appreciate wrongfulness and refrain from certain impulses. A hallmark of the serial murderer is conscious recognition of the illegality of his actions. All the while, he conducts his predatory lifestyle with continued concerns regarding avoidance of detection. So, he is no less alleviated of responsibility than is the antisocial personality, who also continues his criminal ways regardless of existing laws and is not exempt from culpability. Precautions such as Dahmer's security system, Gacy and Nilsen's disposal methods, or other offenders' proud display of bodies for authorities to find are not behaviors of people unable to recognize the wrongfulness of their actions.

It makes sense that a diagnostic manual that recognizes patterns such as pathological gambling and intermittent explosive disorder should include this virtually clear-cut set of behaviors. This category would be described and defined much like any other syndrome found in the *DSM-IV*. A suggested diagnostic category, named *Homicidal Pattern Disorder*, and which should be listed under "Impulse-Control Disorders Not Elsewhere Classified," (American Psychiatric Association, 1994, p. 269), is detailed in Figure 8.1. The accompanying discussions of etiology would include issues such as biology and environment, as well as sexual dysfunction, intimacy and esteem difficulty, and dissociative process.

A Theory of Violence

The diathesis-stress model combining predisposition and environment is a currently credible theory regarding other mental conditions (e.g., schizophrenia) and is compatible with the most recent studies regarding predisposition and violence. This model can also be applied to the serial killer, initially on an intuitive level but later reinforced by evidence of organic differences among the killers and their dysfunctional heritages.

Figure 8.1
Suggested *DSM* Diagnostic Listing for Homicidal Pattern Disorder

312.40 Homicidal Pattern Disorder
  A. Deliberate and purposeful murder or attempts at murder of strangers on more than one occasion.
  B. Tension or affective arousal at some time before the act.
  C. Pleasure, gratification, or relief in commission or reflection of the acts.
  D. Personality traits consistent with diagnosis of at least one Cluster B Personality Disorder (antisocial, borderline, histronic, narcissistic)
  E. Understanding the illegality of actions and continuation to avoid apprehension.
  F. Murders not motivated by monetary gain, to conceal criminal activity, to express anger or vengeance, in response to a delusion or hallucination, or as a result of impaired judgment (e.g., in dementia, mental retardation, substance intoxication).

Many individuals have difficult, even traumatic childhoods. However, most do not develop into serial killers. The continued stressors of social inadequacy and sexual dysfunction serve only to exacerbate the situation. It follows that there must be an additional element—a ticking bomb waiting go off.

The consistent appearance of extreme sexual dysfunction could be taken in an even greater context than is afforded by this study. An argument could be made that sexual motivation is the single most crucial factor in the development of a serial killer. Other factors may reduce the "natural" checks and balances in a person's life to dissuade him from killing, for whatever reason. However, sexual desires initiate patterns in a person's habits, and cyclical behaviors to fulfill one's desires can be reduced, albeit simplistically, to acts of killing for sex.

This possibility is echoed by Masters (1993), in regard to Dennis Nilsen:

If Nilsen's crimes could be explained in terms of distortion of the sexual need, that might provide sufficient answer in itself. There is certainly no lack of precedents, and any experienced prostitute will confirm that the varieties of sexual stimulation are seemingly endless. (p. 256)

However, we must resist the temptation to label the serial killer as just an extreme collector of sexual paraphilia: The explanation is too simplistic. Kemper's early homicides, Dahmer's obsessions with dead things, as well as many other examples found in the literature preclude the supposition that serial killers kill simply for sex. The relief of tension and the feeling of ultimate control and possession play too great a role.

Stanton E. Samenow underscored the importance of a predeterminant when he stated that criminals who claim they were rejected by everyone of importance in their lives rarely say why (Martingale, 1993). Samenow suggests that it is the criminals who reject their parents, rather than vice-versa. He goes on to say, "We ought not to limit our inquiries to what parents have done to children but strive to determine what children have done their parents" (pp. 153–54). It is then noted that Kemper was freely fantasizing by the time he was incarcerated in the basement, he cut the head and hands off his sister's doll long before puberty, and at age 7 said about the teacher he had a crush on: "If I kiss her, I would have to kill her first" (Martingale, 1993, p. 154).

In an interview, the FBI's John Douglas (1995) asserted the serial killer is "born, not made." Florida psychologist Ann McMillan concurs when noting that Gerald Stano, who murdered thirty-five women, was fostered at 6 months, raised by a loving couple, and still turned out to be a monster. She observed, "Sometimes it's not going to matter who raises them. If the parents were Mary and Joseph, it would still turn out the same" (Martingale, 1993, p. 154).

This raises another key point. This theory cannot be viewed with each factor always carrying the same weight. Stano's possible biological pre-disposition may be so great that even just being adopted or some sexual perversions can lead to murder. DeSalvo and Lucas's environments could have held much more weight. Sadistic sex in the case of Kemper and Chikatilo was very important, but sex appeared to be much less of a factor to Des Nilsen, who was obsessed with loneliness and social isolation. However, the appearance of both biological abnormality of some kind and environmental trauma is an established pattern.

The degree to which certain factors figure in the development of these killers does appear to vary. However, problems of personality, retreat to fantasy and dissociation, control-based problems, and sexual dysfunction all are there in some form or another.

Additionally, these case histories dealt with the issue of prior crimes, highlighting the importance and significance of them in each individual's development. The fetish burglaries, the flashings, the pedophilia, and the paraphilia are often signals of bad things to come. Sexual control and obsession themes are red flags for the serial killer. Psychiatrist Robert Brittain (1970) noted: "When sadistic murderers are finally caught, their criminal histories usually reveal they have committed sex offenses of a non-violent nature" (p. 10) and that this type offender should be closely monitored in the future.

The Irreplaceable Dimension of Intuition

The theory proposed in this book is admittedly an intuitive assimilation, resulting from case studies and analysis of the literature. The analysis provides clear examples of the constructs, but must be understood in the context of this study's limitations. Surely, four cases hardly are statistically significant, but when examined in light of available information, are representative of the population described as serial murderers.

Canter, (1994) considered the criticisms of intuitive research, and stated:

As in all intuition, there are recognizable sources that can be brought to the surface for examination and development . . . sensitivity to detail . . . ability to perceive patterns . . . background knowledge with which patterns can be compared. . . . Scientists, though, need intuition too, but are afraid to take it at face value . . . but they be free of intuition. The whole basis of the scientific enterprise is faith that patterns will be found, results will be forthcoming from ideas that have never been asked to stand up to test. This is especially true of psychology when it is believed that ways of thinking about human behavior and experience will reveal shapes and structures that will increase our understanding. The FBI's Behavioral Science Unit strengthened that faith: there were patterns there; the shadows cast by criminals were not arbitrary; they could be read. (pp. 73, 76)

The shadows of the serial murderer have been read. It is possible to recognize the pattern, the individual, and some of the ingredients. With further study it may be possible to avoid, if not predict, some of the instances of this criminality and thereby lessen its terrible impact upon the society in which he lives.

Appendix A

Case Briefs

Berdella, Robert 1984–1988, Missouri. Kidnapped, sadistically raped, tortured, and killed six men. Cut up bodies and put out with trash, keeping various trophies. Confessed and sentenced to life.

Berkowitz, David 1976–1977, New York. The "Son of Sam," shot thirteen men and women on eight occasions, six fatally. Attacked victims while parked in cars at night. Unsuccessfully attempted insanity defense, stating demon-possessed dogs ordered him to kill.

Bianchi, Kenneth/Buono, Angelo 1977–1978, California and Washington. The "Hillside Stranglers," raped, tortured, and killed eleven women, dumping the corpses along the highways. Bianchi attempted an elaborate faking of a multiple personality in his defense, but was uncovered and convicted, along with Buono.

Bittaker, Lawrence/Norris, Roy 1979, California. The sadistic pair met in prison and planned to rape and kill a girl of each age from 13 to 19. Convicted of five killings, they were believed responsible for many more. Bodies were found brutally mutilated. Norris testified against Bittaker and received forty-five years to life, while Bittaker got a death sentence plus 199 years.

Brudos, Jerry 1968–1969, Oregon. Fueled by a long history of foot fetishes and revenge toward women, he sexually assaulted, tortured, and killed four women. He often took pictures and kept severed feet to dress in spiked heels.

Bundy, Ted 1974–1978, various states. One of the highest-profile serial killers ever, he thoroughly enjoyed his fame and notoriety, up to his execution in 1989. Numbers of victims may have reached fifty, as the attractive law student lured women wherever he went. His final rampage, an uncharacteristic set of impulse killings, led to his final arrest. He acted as his attorney, reveling in the attention before his eventual conviction and death sentence.

Buono, Angelo. *See* Bianchi

Chase, Richard 1978, California. The "Vampire Killer," fueled by a schizophrenic belief he needed to drink blood, butchered and mutilated six victims in their homes. A classic disorganized offender, he was the subject of one of the earliest successful attempts by the FBI to utilize psychological profiling.

Chikatilo, Andrei. *See* Case Studies, Chapter 5

Corll, Dean 1970–1973, Texas. With the help of two cohorts who procured young males for him, he sexually abused, tortured, and killed at least twenty-seven. He was eventually killed by one of his partners, Wayne Henley, after Corll threatened to shoot him.

Corona, Juan 1971, California. Diagnosed schizophrenic in 1956, he was accused of the homosexual assaults and murders of twenty-five men after the bodies were found in shallow graves near his home. He was convicted in 1982 after an earlier conviction was overturned.

Dahmer, Jeffery. *See* Case Studies, Chapter 5

DeSalvo, Albert 1962–1964, Massachusetts. The "Boston Strangler," after an extensive past of breaking and entering and countless sexual assaults, he conned his way into women's homes, murdered thirteen, and ritualistically desecrated the corpses. He confessed while in a mental institution and was eventually murdered in prison.

Dodd, Westley Alan 1989, Washington and Oregon. A prolific sadistic pedophile, he killed three young children and was stopped only when caught attempting to abduct another child. He kept a detailed diary, complete with torture and killing methods. In 1993, he became the first in thirty years to be executed by hanging.

Eyler, Larry 1982–1984, various states. Suspected in at least twenty-two other murders, he was finally convicted of the killing, torture, and dismemberment of a 15-year-old boy whose body parts were dumped out with the trash. He was the prototypical self-hating homosexual, macho acting while torturing and killing other homosexual men. He was given a death sentence.

Fish, Albert 1910–1934, various states. This aging pervert took great pride in his extensive experience in sadism, inflicting and receiving pain. He killed and ate a 10-year-old girl and cruelly wrote the parents six years later with details of the crime. He was executed in 1936 at age 65, claiming to anticipate it with glee.

Gacy, John Wayne 1972–1978, Illinois. Another high-profile killer, the "Killer Clown" had a history of psychiatric and sexual problems, eventually culminating in thirty-three murders. A pillar of the community, he lured young men to his home with parties and promises of employment, then sodomized, tortured, and killed them. He buried twenty-nine under his house. He was executed in 1994.

Gein, Ed 1954–1957, Wisconsin. Used as a model for the movies *Psycho* and *Silence of the Lambs*, he dug up female bodies for experiments and collection of parts. He killed two women who reminded him of his mother. He was declared criminally insane and died in an institution in 1984.

Heirens, William 1945–1946, Illinois. The "Lipstick Killer" murdered three in their homes, including a 6-year-old girl whose body was dismembered. He was diagnosed as a sexual psychopath with maniacal tendencies and tried to blame an imaginary alter-ego named George. After receiving three life sentences, he became the first Illinois prison inmate to be awarded a college degree.

Jack the Ripper 1888, England. At least five savage butcheries were attributed to this earliest of serial killers. His disemboweled victims were usually accompanied by cheerful notes signed by his famous nickname. A unsubstantiated diary published in 1993 contained many convincing documents and caused great dispute.

Joubert, John 1982–1983, Nebraska. Killed and mutilated three young boys. Subsequently requested crime scene photos to enjoy in his cell. Sentenced to death.

Kearney, Patrick 1968–1977, California. Dubbed the "Trash Bag Killer" for his disposal methods of dismembered victims, he killed between twenty-eight and forty, mostly homosexual men. He received two life sentences after signing twenty-eight confessions.

Kemper, Edmund. *See* Case Studies, Chapter 5

Long, Bobby Joe 1984, Florida. Cruising in his car, he abducted, assaulted, and murdered at least ten young women. He had an extensive history of physical abnormalities and trauma. After confessing, he received twenty-six life sentences and two death sentences.

Lucas, Henry Lee/Toole, Ottis 1970–1983, various states. Convicted of ten killings, Lucas and Toole claimed at one time to have killed at least three hundred and sixty victims across the country, with stories often changing. Victims varied in ages, most were white females, sexually assaulted at some point. Killing methods also varied.

Mudgett, Herman 1893–1896, Pennsylvania and various states. After creating a three-story row of conjoined buildings, he turned them into an elaborate death and torture chamber. He killed anywhere between twenty and one hundred, including men, women, and children, and even sold some of the cadavers to a medical school. He was hanged in 1896.

Nance, Wayne 1974–1986, Montana. The baby-faced deliveryman gained access to people's homes through his job, murdering six and collecting mementos along the way. After developing an obsession with a female coworker, he attacked her and her husband at their home, and was eventually killed in a wild gun battle.

Nilsen, Dennis 1978–1983, England. The lonely homosexual often paralleled with Jeffery Dahmer, killed sixteen men "for company." He was discovered when the cut up body parts he flushed down the toilet started backing up. He received life in prison.

Norris, Roy. *See* Bittaker

Ramirez, Richard 1984–1985, California. The infamous "Night Stalker" was unique among serial killers, in that the only thing linking the victims was that they were killed in their homes. He killed, raped, mutilated, and pillaged indiscriminately. His Satanic connection was believed less important than his enjoyment for killing. He was found eligible for the death penalty.

Rifkin, Joel 1989–1993, New York. During a routine traffic stop, he was discovered to have the corpse of a victim in his pickup truck. He finally confessed to seventeen killings, mostly prostitutes.

Rissell, Monte 1975–1976, various states. Raped twelve, killed five women before the age of 19. He kept trophies and attacked victims of all types, fueled by a hatred of women.

Rogers, Dayton Leroy 1984–1987, Oregon. A mild-mannered, respected businessman, he killed eight women, reveling in bondage and mutilation. He was caught after slashing to death his last victim in plain view. Sentenced to death by lethal injection.

Rolling, Danny 1989–1990, Florida. A Ted Bundy fan, he decided to kill eight people for each year he served in prison. After three murders the prior year, he killed five Gainesville-area college students, raping three, mutilating, and posing their bodies. He was already serving four life sentences in Florida State Prison when he was sentenced to death in the electric chair.

Shawcross, Arthur. *See* Case Studies, Chapter 5

Stano, Gerald 1969–1983, Florida. Confessed to twenty-five killings of young women, possibly linked to forty or more. Sexual assaults after death. Born to a mother who lost five children owing to abuse and neglect.

Toole, Ottis. *See* Lucas

Wuornos, Aileen 1989–1990, Florida. A lesbian drifter, she fueled her hunts with alcohol and a mounting rage against men. She killed at least seven along the Florida interstates, luring them with promises of sex and hard-luck stories. She eventually confessed and was convicted and sentenced to death in 1992.

Zwanziger, Anna 1809, Bavaria. Convicted of poisoning two women and a child, she regarded arsenic as her "truest friend." She was executed two years later.

Appendix B

Explanation of Terms

It is necessary to define exactly what is meant by the terms used this book. There is little agreement among researchers regarding many of the issues discussed here, let alone the meaning of each term. Therefore, the following explains how each term is used in the context of this book.

Clinically antisocial behavior: Behavior possibly described within the psychiatric community as more problematic than is found in the average person's usual process of growing up. This includes features of the MacDonald triad—namely, animal abuse, late enuresis, and fire setting. It also includes behavior clusters recognized by the *DSM-IV*, such as childhood, adolescent, or adult antisocial behavior, sociopathology, and other disorders.

Dissociative episodes: Displays of a temporary loss of consciousness or withdrawal within the subject's own mind. The term is closely related to flights of fantasy, and an individual's becoming deeply immersed in fantasy is considered a dissociative episode.

Early age: Refers to the subject's age before turning 18, although emotional immaturity can cloud this distinction. The idea is to recognize moments of development that can be viewed as irregular. The MacDonald triad of behaviors occurs at an early numeric age, but lesser crimes committed prior to the beginning of a murderous pattern may also apply.

Environmental trauma: Any out-of-the-ordinary activity the subject may have experienced when growing up. This term is reasonably close to universal, applying to essentially the general population and including, experiences ranging from those that damage a person's developing ego to those that render the person deeply disturbed and even dangerous.

Evidence: The appearance, at least once, of an incident in the case history of a subject. This does not indicate there is or was only one incident of whatever is being discussed, only that some instance has been noted in the study. When there are several instances of a particular nature, it is noted, as well as is minimal appearance of said instance. However, there are no set parameters regarding minimum and maximum occurrences.

Lesser (or early) crimes: Crimes committed prior to the subject's first serial murder, usually such as breaking and entering, or arson, and may include serious offenses as well.

MacDonald triad: A three-pronged set of behaviors in youth, that indicate a developing antisocial or pathological personality. The theory was postulated by MacDonald in 1963 and Hellman and Blackman in 1966. The behaviors include enuresis (late bed-wetting), fire setting, and cruelty to animals.

Mass murderer: The FBI's term to describe an offender who kills multiple victims in basically a single episode—such as, a sniper or a shooter killing indiscriminately at a public location. This offender usually displays an overt mental imbalance and is the emotional opposite of the serial killer, described in this book as a cold, calculated predator.

Physiological anomalies: Any physical or biological marker or event that could label the subject physically different from what is considered average. These could include actual physical injury, illness, vitamin deficiency, genetic makeup, chromosomal or chemical measurements, or conditions connected to a genetic link or disposition; also, evidence of certain aspects of the family that suggest factors of heredity and predisposition.

Predatory murders: Murders committed in a calculated, selective manner with no apparent motive other than the killer's enjoyment. Killings may be driven by interest in sadism or sex, but not by reasons rendering the murder incidental, such as monetary gain.

Problematic: A relative term, similar to *severe*, refers to a factor's impact on the subject's life and its importance within that individual's context.

Serial, serial killer: Repetitive, cyclical activity, usually associated with a buildup of tension, committing the crime, and a cooling-off period. Actual numbers are unimportant; what is relevant is the compulsion to repetitively commit the crime. The only reason Andrei Chikatilo had fifty more kills than Westley Alan Dodd was because Dodd was caught earlier in his career. (This also precludes the mass murderer or spree killer, as the serial killer's interest in murder is a continual, life-long obsessive cycle.)

Severe: A subjective term, refers to whether something may have affected the subject excessively, within the individual's context. For example, many 18-year-olds may not have been excessively distressed when left on their own, but for Jeffery Dahmer it may have been too much for his already fragile psyche.

Usually, severity is self-explanatory and applicable to the majority of the population, so exceptions are be noted and explained.

Sexual deviance: Any sexual preference, interest, or obsession that could be considered out of the ordinary and problematic, where it interferes with the individual's functioning in daily life. For example, a foot fetish becomes deviant and problematic when it leads to fetish burglaries and assaults; homosexuality becomes deviant and problematic when the subject develops a loathing for himself and others like him.

Spree killer: An FBI term referring to offenders who go on a rampage of crime, often including multiple murders, but usually during an extension of one basic episode. The description may encompass more time than the frenzied explosion of typical mass murderer, however. This offender differs from the serial killer in time of activity and emotional disposition.

References

Abdo, J. (1994). Jury returns unanimous sentence for Rolling. *Independent Florida Alligator, 87,* (137), 1.

Abel, G. G., & Blanchard, E. B. (1974). The role of fantasy in the treatment of sexual deviation. *Archives of General Psychiatry, 30,* 467–475.

A horror warning for Dahmer trial. (1992). *Chicago Sun Times,* January 28, p. 14.

American Psychiatric Association. (1987). *Diagnostic and statistical manual of mental disorders* (3rd ed.). Washington, DC: American Psychiatric Association.

American Psychiatric Association. (1994). *Diagnostic and statistical manual of mental disorders, quick reference guide* (4th ed.). Washington, DC: American Psychiatric Association.

Andreasen, N. C. (1984). *The broken brain: The biological revolution in psychiatry.* New York: Harper & Row.

Apsche, J. A. (1993). *Probing the mind of a serial killer.* Morrisville, PA: International Information Association.

Bandura, A. (1969). *Principles of behavior modification.* New York: Holt, Rinehart & Winston.

Behavioral genetics. (1982). New York: Research and Education Association.

Bliss, E. C. (1986). *Multiple personality, allied disorders & hypnosis.* New York: Oxford University Press.

Brittain, R. P. (1970). The sadistic murderer. *Medicine, Science and the Law, 10.*

Bruno, F. J. (1993). *Psychological symptoms.* New York: John Wiley.

Burgess, A. W., Hartman, C. R., & Ressler, R. K. (1986). Sexual homicide: a motivational model. *Journal of Interpersonal Violence, 1*, 251–272.

Cahill, T. (1986). *Buried dreams*. New York: Bantam Books.

Campbell, D. T., & Stanley, J. C. (1963). *Experimental and quasi experimental designs for research*. Chicago: Rand McNally.

Canter, D. (1994). *Criminal shadows*. Hammersmith, London: HarperCollins.

Cartel, M. (1985). *Disguise of sanity: Serial mass murder*. Toluca Lake, CA: Pepperbox Books.

Casey, M. D., Segall, L. J., Street, D.R.K., & Blank, C. E. (1966). Sex chromosome abnormalities in two state hospitals for patients requiring special security. *Nature, 209*, 641.

Castaneda, C. J. (1993a). 2 pictures emerge of teens accused in slayings. *USA Today*, May 22, p. 1D.

Castaneda, C. J. (1993b). Report: Rituals of rape, death in mutilation case. *USA Today*, June 11, p. 1D.

Cheney, M. (1992). *Why—The serial killer in America*. Saratoga, CA: R & E Publishers.

Chin, P., & Tamarkin, C. (1991). The door of evil. *People*, August 12, p. 34.

Cleckley, H. (1941). *Mask of sanity*. Saint Louis: C. V. Mosby.

Costello, T. W., & Costello, J. T. (1992). *Abnormal psychology*. New York: HarperCollins.

Coston, J. (1992). *To kill and kill again*. New York: Penguin Books.

Court-Brown, W. M., Price, W. H., & Jacobs, P. A. (1968). The XYY male. *British Medical Journal*, 513.

Cullen, R. (1993). *The killer department*. New York: Pantheon Books.

Dahmer, L. (1994). *A father's story*. New York: William Morrow.

Dahmer is given life in prison. (1992). *Boston Globe*, February 18, p. 3.

Davids, D. (1992). The serial murderer as superstar. *McCalls*, February, p. 150.

Davis, D. (1991). *The Milwaukee murders*. New York: St. Martin's Press.

Denzin, N. K. (1970). *Sociological methods: A sourcebook*. Chicago: Aldine.

Denzin, N. K. (1978). *The research act*. New York: McGraw-Hill.

Dietz, P. E. (1992a). *Statement in reaction to Dahmer verdict*.

Dietz, P. E. (1992b). Court testimony at trial of Jeffery Dahmer. *Court TV*, February 12.

Dietz, P. E., Harry, B., & Hazelwood, R. R. (1986). Detective magazines: Pornography for the sexual sadist? *Journal of Forensic Sciences, 31*, (1), 197–211.

Dietz, P. E., Hazelwood, R. R., & Warren, J. W. (1989). The sexually sadistic criminal & his offenses. *Bulletin of the American Academy and the Law*. 1–39.

Dodd, W. A. (1992). *When you meet a stranger*. Unpublished pamphlet.

Douglas, J. (1995) *Day and Date* (November 8).

Douglas, J. E., Ressler, R. K., Burgess, A. W., & Hartman, C. R. (1986). Criminal profiling from crime scene analysis. *Behavioral Sciences & the Law, 4,* (4), 367–393.

Durham III, A. M. (1986). Pornography, social harm and legal control: Observations on Bart. *Justice Quarterly, Academy of Criminal Justice Sciences, 3,* (1), 95–102.

Dutch family provides new proof of genetic link to behavior. (1993). *Springfield (IL) State Journal-Register,* October 25, p. 18.

Dvorchak, R. J., & Holewa, L. (1991). *Milwaukee massacre.* New York: Dell Publishing.

Editors of Time-Life Books. (1992). *Serial killers.* Richmond, VA: Time-Life Books.

Eftimiates, M. (1993). *Garden of graves.* New York: St. Martin's Press.

Egger, S. A. (1985). "Serial murder and the law enforcement response." Unpublished dissertation, College of Criminal Justice, Sam Houston State University, Huntsville, TX.

Egger, S. A. (1990). *Serial murder: An elusive phenomenon.* New York: Praeger.

Elias, M. (1994). Violence is linked to brain deficiency. *USA Today,* July 19, p. 8D.

Ellroy, J. (1991). *Murder & mayhem.* Lincolnwood, IL: Publications International.

Ewing, C. P. (1990). *Kids who kill.* New York: Avon.

Expert tells of Dahmer's twisted acts. (1992). *Boston Herald-American,* February 5, p. 3.

Federal Bureau of Investigation. (1985). The men who murdered, The split reality of murder. *Law Enforcement Bulletin,* 1–11.

Frank, G. (1967). *The Boston strangler.* New York: Signet.

Freud, S. (1938). *Splitting of the ego in the process of defense.* Standard Edition, 23, 271–278.

Fromm, E. (1973). *The anatomy of human destructiveness.* New York: Holt, Rinehart & Winston.

Garelik, G., & Maranto, G. (1984). Multiple murderers. *Discover,* p. 28.

Gibbons, D. C. (1987). *Society, crime & criminal behavior.* Englewood Cliffs, NJ: Prentice-Hall.

Glaser, B., & Strauss, A. L. (1967). *The discovery of grounded theory.* Chicago: Aldine.

Gottesman, I. I., & Shields, J. (1982). *Schizophrenia: The epigenetic puzzle.* Cambridge, MA: Cambridge University Press.

Grossman, W. (1991). Pain, aggression, fantasy & concepts of sadomasochism. *Psychoanalytic Quarterly, 60,* 22–52.

Grotstein, J. S. (1979). The soul in torment: An older and newer view of psychopathology. *Bulletin of the National Council of Catholic Psychologists, 25,* 36–52.

Hans, S., & Marcus, J. (1987). A process model for the development of schizophrenia. *Psychiatry: Interpersonal and Biological Processes, 50*, 361–370.

Hare, R. (1991). *Manual for the revised psychopathy checklist.* Toronto: Multi-Health Systems.

Hare, R. (1993). *Without Conscience: The disturbing world of the psychopaths among us.* New York: Pocket Books.

Hare, R., McPherson, L., & Forth, A. (1988). Male psychopaths & their criminal careers. *Journal of Consulting Clinical Psychology, 56*, 710–714.

Harper's biochemistry, 22nd ed. (1990). Norwalk, CT: Appleton & Lange.

Harrison, S., & Barrett, M. (1993). *The diary of Jack the Ripper: The discovery, the investigation, the debate.* New York: Hyperion. first published in Great Britain by Smith Gryphon Limited.

Havens, R. (1992), personal communication.

Hazelwood, R., & Douglas, J. (1980). The lust murderer. *FBI Law Enforcement Bulletin*, April.

Hellman, D., & Blackman, N. (1966). Enuresis, firesetting, and cruelty to animals. *American Journal of Psychiatry, 122*, 1431–1435.

Hickey, E. W. (1991). *Serial murderers and their victims.* Pacific Grove, CA: Brooks-Cole.

Holmes, R. M., & DeBurger, J. (1988). *Serial murder.* Newbury Park, CA: Sage.

Inside Edition. (1993). Interviews with Jeffery Dahmer and Richard Ramirez.

Jackman, T., & Cole, T. (1992). *Rites of burial.* New York: Windsor.

Jacobs, P. A., Brunton, M., & Melville, M. M. (1965). Aggressive behavior, mental subnormality and the XYY male. *Nature*, 1351.

Jaffe, P., Wolfe, D., Wilson, S., & Zak, L. (1986). Similarities in behavioral and social maladjustment among child victims and witnesses to family violence. *American Journal of Orthopsychiatry, 56*, 142–146.

Juror: Dahmer is a con artist. (1992). *Springfield (IL) State Journal Register*, February 16, p. 1.

Kendall, E. (1981). *The phantom prince: My life with Ted Bundy.* Seattle: Madrona.

King, G. C. (1992). *Blood lust.* New York: Penguin Books.

King, G. C. (1993). *Driven to kill.* New York: Pinnacle Books.

Kohut, H. (1971). *Analysis of the self.* New York: International Universities Press.

Kraus, R. T. (1995). An enigmatic personality: Case report of a serial killer. *Journal of Orthomolecular Medicine, 10*, (1), 11–24.

Krivich, M., & Ol'gin, O. (1993). *Comrade Chikatilo: The psychopathology of Russia's most notorious serial killer.* Fort Lee, NJ: Barricade Books.

Levin, J., & Fox, J. A. (1985). *Mass murder: America's growing menace.* New York: Plenum Press.

Lewine, R.R.J., Gulley, L. R., Risch, S. C., Jewart, R., & Houpt, J. (1990). Sexual dimorphism, brain morphology and schizophrenia. *Schizophrenia Bulletin, 16*, (2), 195–203.

Leyton, E. (1986). *Hunting humans: Inside the minds of mass murderers*. New York: Pocket Books.

Lifton, R. J. (1986). *The Nazi doctors*. New York: Basic Books.

Lincoln, Y. S., & Guba, A. L. (1985). *Naturalistic inquiry*. Beverly Hills, CA: Sage Publications.

Lindsey, R. (1984). Officials cite a rise in killers who roam the US for victims. *New York Times*, January 21, pp. 1,7.

Lourie, R. (1993). *Hunting the devil*. New York: HarperCollins.

MacCulloch, M. J., Snowdon, P. R., & Wood, P.J.W. (1983). Sadistic fantasy, sadistic behaviour & offending. *British Journal of Psychiatry, 143*, 20–29.

MacDonald, J. (1963). The threat to kill. *American Journal of Psychiatry, 120*, 125–130.

Man reportedly confesses to 17 murders. (1993). *Springfield (IL) State-Journal Register*, June 29, p. 3.

Martingale, M. (1993). *Cannibal killers: The history of impossible murderers*. New York: Carroll & Graf Publishers.

Masters, B. (1991). Dahmer's inferno. *Vanity Fair*, November, p. 269.

Masters, B. (1993). *Killing for company*. New York: Random House.

McKay, S. (1985). Coming to grips with random killers. *MacLean's*, July 8, pp. 44–45.

Mellish, P. (1989). Serial killers & porn. *The Backlash Times*. p. 5.

Meloy, J. R. (1988). *The psychopathic mind: origins, dynamics, & treatment*. Northvale, NJ: Jason Aronson.

Meloy, J. R. (1992). *Violent attachments*. Northvale, NJ: Jason Aronson.

Meloy, J. R. (1993). *Assessment of violence potential: The psychopathic personality*. Seminars held in St. Louis, MO, June 7 & 8.

Milwaukee Police Department. (1991). *Homicide incident report: Jeffery Dahmer's arrest and subsequent confession*. Milwaukee Police.

Money, J. (1970). Behavior genetics: Principles, methods and examples from XO, XXY and XYY syndromes. *Seminar in Psychiatry, 2*, 11.

Moyer, K. E. (1968). *Kinds of aggression and their biological basis. Communication in behavioral biology*, (vol. 2), New York: Academic.

Neilsen, J. (1970). Criminality among patients with Kleinfelter's syndrome and the XYY syndrome. *British Journal of Psychiatry, 117*, 365.

Neilsen, J., Tsuboi, T., Turver., B., Jensen, J. T., & Sachs, J. (1969). Prevalence and incidence of the XYY syndrome and Kleinfelter's syndrome in an institution for criminal psychopaths. Horsens, *Denmark. Acta Psychiat. Scand., 45*, 402.

Newton, M. (1990). *Hunting humans*. New York: Avon Books.

Norris, J. (1992). *Walking time bombs*. New York: Bantam Books.

O'Brien, D. (1985). *Two of a kind: The Hillside stranglers*. New York: Penguin Books.

Olsen, J. (1993). *The misbegotten son*. New York: Delacorte Press.

O'Reilly, P. O., Hughes, R. T., Russell, S., & Ernest, M. B. (1965). The mauve factor: An evaluation. *Diseases of the Nervous System, 26*, 562.

Pervin, L. A. (1989). *Personality: Theory & research*. New York: John Wiley.

Pfeiffer, C. C. (1974). Observations on the therapy of the schizophrenias. *Journal of Applied Nutrition, 26*, (4), 29.

Pfeiffer, C. C., Sohler, A., Jenny, C. H., & Iliev, V. (1974). Treatment of pyroluric schizophrenia and a dietary supplement of zinc. *Journal of Orthomolecular Psychiatry, 3*, (4), 1.

Prentky, R. A., Burgess, A. W., Rokous, F., Lee, A., Harman, C., Ressler, R., & Douglas, J. (1989). The presumptive role of fantasy in serial sexual homicide. *American Journal of Psychiatry, 146*, (7), 887–891.

Price, W. H., & Jacobs, P. A. (1970). The 47,XYY male with special reference to behavior. *Seminars in Psychiatry, 117*, 365.

Price, W. H., & Whatmore, P. B. (1967). Behavior disorder and patterns of crime among XYY males identified at a maximum security hospital. *British Medical Journal, 1*, 533.

Prince, M. (1975). *Psychotherapy & multiple personality: Selected essays*. Cambridge, MA: Harvard University Press.

Reinhardt, J. J. (1992). *Sex perversions & sex crimes*. Springfield, IL: Charles C. Thomas.

Ressler, R. (1992). *Whoever fights monsters*. New York: St. Martin's Press.

Ressler, R., Burgess, R. K., D'Agostino, R. & Douglas, J. E. (1984). "Serial murder: A new phenomenon of homicide." Paper presented at the annual meeting of the International Association of Forensic Sciences, Oxford, England.

Revitch, E., & Schlesinger, L. B. (1981). *The psychopathology of homicide*. Springfield, IL: Charles C. Thomas.

Reynolds, M. (1992). *Dead ends*. New York: Warner Books.

Sears, D. J. (1991). *To kill again: The motivation and development of serial murder*. Wilmington, DE: Scholarly Resources.

2nd Boston strangler eyed. (1993). *Boston Herald*. May 17, p. 3.

Sievers, D. (1992). personal communication.

Silverton, L., Mednick, S., Schulsinger, F., Parnas, J., & Harrington, M. (1988). Genetic risk for schizophrenia, birthweight, & cerebral ventricular enlargement. *Journal of Abnormal Psychology, 97*, 4, 496–498.

Sloan, M. P., & Meyer, J. H. (1983). Typology for parents of abused children. *Child Abuse and Neglect, 7*, 443–450.

Smith, S. R., & Meyer, R. G. (1987). *Law, behavior & mental health: Policy & practice*. New York: New York University Press.

Snider, M. (1993). Genetic flaw makes some men violent. *USA Today*, October 22, p. 1D.

Solotaroff, I. (1993). The terrible secret of Citizen Ch. *Esquire*, pp. 95–99.

Sproull, N. L. (1988). *Handbook of research methods: A guide for practitioners and students in the social sciences.* Metuchen, NJ: Scarecrow Press.

Studies find link between gene and personality. (1996), *Springfield (IL) State Journal-Register,* January 2, p. 1.

Toufexis, A. (1992). Do mad acts a madman make? *Time,* February 3, p. 17.

Toufexis, A. (1995). Monster mice. *Time,* December 4, p. 76.

Walker, E., Downey, G., & Bergman, A., (1989). The effects of parental psychopathology and maltreatment on child behavior: A test of the diathesis-stress model. *Child Development, 60,* 15–24.

Ward, J. L. (1975). Relationship of kryptopyrrole, zinc and pyridoxine in schizophrenia. *Journal of Orthomolecular Psychiatry, 4,* 27.

West, D. J. (1987). *Sexual crimes and confrontations: A study of victims and offenders.* Brookfield, VT: Gower.

Wilson, C. (1989). *Written in blood: The criminal mind and method.* New York: Warner Books.

Wilson, C., & Seaman, D. (1991). *The serial killers: A study in the psychology of violence.* Washington, DC: U.S. Department of Justice.

Witness: Dahmer said he'd "eat my heart." (1992). *Springfield (IL) State Journal-Register,* February 1, p. 3.

Yin, R. K. (1984). *Case study research: Design & methods.* Thousand Oaks, CA: Sage.

Zeuthen, E., Hansen, M., Christensen, A. L., & Neilsen, J. (1975). A psychiatric-psychological study of XYY males found in a general male population. *Acta Psychiat. Scand. 51,* 3–18.

Index

About the Author

STEPHEN J. GIANNANGELO is a Special Agent with the Illinois Department of Revenue, Bureau of Criminal Investigation. He is currently a member of the Illinois State Police Task Force on financial and white-collar crime. He holds a master's degree in Forensic Psychology from the University of Illinois at Springfield.

ISBN 0-275-95434-X

90000>

EAN

9 780275 954345

HARDCOVER BAR CODE